Lonely Boy

Musings on Death, Mental Health and Relationships

by
Daragh Fleming

Interior Formatting: Dorothy Dreyer
Cover Design: Jason O'Gorman
Edited by Niall MacGiolla Bhuí, TheDocCheck.Com

Published by Book Hub Publishing, An Independent
Publishing House, Galway and Limerick, Ireland.
www.bookhubpublishing.com

ISBN: 978-1-7391012-8-2

Table of Contents

"I will keep constant watch over myself and —most usefully — will put each day up for review. For this is what makes us evil — that none of us looks back upon our own lives. We reflect upon only that which we are about to do. And yet our plans for the future descend from the past."
- Seneca, Moral Letters

For *The Lonely Boys*

Foreword

Daragh Fleming's honest portrayal of mental health, wellbeing and recovery opens with a quote from Seneca, Moral Letters that states: 'I will keep constant watch over myself.' Throughout Fleming's 'Lonely Boy', loss, friendship and death are at the forefront, and they are observed with a quiet awareness. It is at times a memoir, at times a guide, but it is always conscious of what it is doing. Fleming, as in life, is keeping a constant watch over his writing and the effect of his words.

Fleming's writing is simple, direct, and incredibly honest. There is a vulnerability to the topics that he deals with, and he does not try to hide from it. Lonely Boy deals with the tragic suicide of a best friend, crippling panic attacks, what it is to be a man and what is expected of dangerous paradigms, the benefits of therapy, among many other pertinent discussions that should happen much more frequently. The writing is intimate and vernacular, so you feel that you might just be in a bar with Daragh where the conversation is flowing easily. By writing this book, in this way, Fleming reveals how these conversations in our society do not flow as easily or as frequently as they should.

At the heart of Lonely Boy is a man trying to be at peace with himself and his past, so that he can navigate his future. By doing this, he opens up about his struggles with mental health and what has worked for him. He is at no point condescending or preachy, but instead welcoming and helpful. He admits that he does not have the answers but by sharing his story with us helps us understand the questions. I'd recommend this book to anyone who has struggled with mental health, to any man who does not feel like he fits in, and to anyone who is open to reflection and growth.

Patrick Holloway

Introduction:
A Note on Being Alone

There's more than one way to be alone. That's a reasonable place to start.

There's good alone-ness and not so good alone-ness, but it's more like a spectrum than a binary distinction. The benefits that come from being alone depends on context, as do the pitfalls. Good alone-ness might be defined as time spent alone out of choice, in order to get some known goal completed -- we might want time to think, or relax, or work, on our own. We can use time spent alone to grow and work on ourselves. After spending long periods of time with other people we regularly crave our own company. We generally call this form solitude. When I think of this version of being alone, I think of Superman, brooding away in his *Fortress of Solitude*, reflecting and deciding on his next moves. It's a very necessary way to spend time. We want for it, and it's important to be able to spend time with yourself without falling into negative thinking. Being able to quietly navigate through your own thoughts without any distractions is an important skill, and one which is rarer than you might think. You on your own, without distractions, and by choice, is the strongest version of who you are.

The other common form of being alone is loneliness, which is a version of alone on the other end of the spectrum, so to speak. You might define loneliness as the unchosen state of being alone. Loneliness results from being alone for too long without desiring to be so. It's a feeling of isolation, and desperation caused by awareness of the fact that you are on your own when you would rather not be. It comes about more often when you don't enjoy your own company, when you want to do anything other than be by yourself. The state of unwanted alone-ness – the alone that isn't chosen – will result in loneliness. All circumstances might be the same as with solitude here, aside from this lack of choice, and this makes all the difference. A cold shower can build resilience when you choose to have one. A cold shower sprung upon you without consent is torture.

The choice to be alone is what separates loneliness from solitude.

However, solitude isn't universally good, and loneliness isn't always bad. Villains brood in solitude too, and the outcomes of their solitude can be devastating. There are countless villains throughout history who've come to heinous decisions due to being left to brood in isolation for too long. Additionally, when we are lonely, we can learn an incredible amount about ourselves, which is invaluable. Although loneliness can be difficult, it can be beneficial. The person who spends unwanted time alone will eventually understand why they may come to dislike their own company, and from this point you can build a better relationship with yourself. Sometimes loneliness is worth suffering through to become a better version of who we are.

We all feel lonely at times. It's not an avoidable feeling, the same way you cannot avoid happiness or sadness. It's not an unnatural state to be in, but it's often an unnatural state to remain in. To me, it acts as a sign that I need to change something. It is the great alarm system of mental distress. If I begin to feel lonely it means I've been neglecting my relationships -- I haven't been seeing enough friends, I haven't called home to the family in some time, I haven't been maintaining the relationship I have with myself. Feeling lonely tells me that I'm beginning to walk in the wrong direction. It's a precursor to mental unwellness.

I can see that now, yes, but I didn't always see it. For years I existed in loneliness, and I never really understood the full effect it was having on me until I took the time to address the issue. Rather than seeing it as a warning sign I saw it as misguided confirmation that there was something wrong with me. I thought that normal people, people who were well adjusted, never felt lonely. As we go on we will see this attitude was a result of the poor relationship I had with myself. I wasn't someone I liked, and I saw loneliness as my personal failure, rather than a sign that I needed to help myself.

Loneliness can wreak havoc on you if you allow it to run amuck unsupervised. You'll start to believe things about yourself, and about others, which aren't true. Sour and bitter thoughts will flood your mind and take over. You'll begin to behave outside of your regular repertoire – you'll feel more anxious, you'll think people no longer like you, you'll do whatever it takes for the fleeting attention of people who neither care nor really matter. You'll find yourself believing things which are clearly untrue in times when you aren't so anxious and paranoid. Oftentimes, you'll give up on the activities you were once passionate about. Loneliness is a brutal experience, but there is a lot to be learned from it. You'll understand yourself more than you ever have if you go through long bouts of isolation, assuming you're brave enough to delve deeper into exactly who you are, and willing to accept the issues which are causing you to become lonely.

This collection of essays is about mental health, and how loneliness affects it. It's about the years I spent in and out of very lonely periods, which were often self-inflicted, and ultimately ignored, for fear of what lay underneath it. I refused to heal from things which had hurt me deep in my past. I chose to be alone and then I couldn't escape from it when I wanted to. I became a prisoner in a cage I had created. I was the sort of person who would push people away and then lament about how alone I was. These reflections address the flaws I was ignoring, as well as the lessons I learned from what I discovered. None of it was easy, but all of it was worthwhile.

In my early and mid-20s I spent hours upon hours alone. Not all of those hours felt lonely, and a lot of them were required for work. Particularly during the years of the pandemic, the time I spent alone became lonely as I compared my aloneness to the togetherness of my closest friends. I'd been on my own for so long that I knew deep down there had to be underlying issues with me. I eventually forced myself to look inward, to face up to my flaws, and to try and accept them. This has been a painful endeavour, and the healing I eventually experienced came at a hefty price. I went through fluctuations of heightened anxiety and depression as I peeled back the layers of the person I showed the world and looked upon the real me – the me who was afraid to commit, the me who was reckless and hurtful and arrogant, the me who didn't take responsibility for anything because I felt that the world owed me something. The real me, the one who is flawed. But also the one who wanted to become better.

This version of me has parts which are ugly and difficult to look at. However, over time, and with patience, I improved. The ugly parts of me were accepted, and the parts which could be worked on were identified, and actively challenged. I grew from loneliness like the first crop after a famine, and I developed as a person. I am still developing in many ways. I'll never stop developing. There's always something to improve. For me the loneliness was going to exist regardless, and so after several years of putting up with it, I made a decision to use the time to DIY my flaws. I began learning about myself so that eventually the time I spent alone would stop feeling so lonesome.

It is difficult to know at times whether the world is flawed and needs changing, or if it us who are flawed and needing to address those issues which we deny ourselves. The world isn't perfect and it never will be, so blaming our problems on the world is the chancer's way out. When we blame the world, we give up, alleviate ourselves from responsibility, and tell ourselves we are victims rather than the reason we have slipped into disrepair. It is up to us to address our own problems. It is no one else's responsibility. If we wish to fix the world, we need to start with ourselves. That's a truism everyone knows until the exact moment it becomes inconvenient.

The thing is, especially towards my mid-20s, I knew I was flawed. I was, and am, flawed in many, terrible ways. There is no shame in admitting this because we're all flawed, despite our best efforts to convince others we aren't. What worked in my favour is that, after years of denial, I was finally able to look at these flaws as they really exist, rather than continuing to make excuses for myself. I could see them for what they were. I could finally see how I was misbehaving, but that didn't necessarily make the behaviours stop.

Knowledge isn't enough. More work is required. What this knowledge did allow me to do was to see myself for who I was in the context of an imperfect world. I could map the odd shapes of who I was. I was an idealist, a realist, and a cynic. I was quite stoic, but I was also deeply lonesome. There was a part of me that was unattached to anything and another part that wanted to be attached entirely. I was arrogant and dismissive and at times self-righteous.

It's important that we take stock of our negative characteristics too, so that we can curtail them when they flare up. We all have these parts of us – the ugly reflections – which we prefer to ignore and leave in the dark. But we'll never know ourselves fully if we don't also know about these fewer flattering sides.

This book isn't an autobiography. The tales of my life are better suited for the countertops of quiet pubs. This book is about mental health. It's a book about learning to address issues, and about accepting imperfections. I wrote these essays to show that we all have things we need to work out, despite how well-adjusted we might appear. Mental health issues aren't always obvious, and many people you know are struggling with something which you have no knowledge of. These issues can build slowly overtime until suddenly, you find yourself in a place where they are preventing you from finding consistent life satisfaction.

These essays and stories are reflections on a period of my life when my mental health fluctuated constantly. At times I was very happy and consistent, but there were also many months where I spiralled downwards into depression and low mood. As I worked through my issues, I began to understand why I was feeling the way I was feeling, and then went on to address the issues that were causing these fluctuations. My hope is that reading about this process will help in some way, and if you are experiencing similar problems, you will be able to begin looking at what might be bothering you, too.

This is a book about addressing flaws. It's also about framing these flaws in the context of the society we have created, and how this society can exaggerate and amplify some of them. Our society tends to sweep any and all problems under the carpet provided by social media, and so many of us don't talk about our faults, let alone think about them. We've been trained to believe that having flaws is wrong and inappropriate, which is a ridiculous position when you exist in an imperfect world. It is quite literally impossible to be alive without imperfections. I don't think any of these flaws are uncommon, but due to social pressures, we're conditioned to express only our positive traits, so many of us will never see ourselves for what we really are – and that is at the very core, flawed people.

Along the way there has been sadness and anxiety, rage and jealousy, guilt and panic, loneliness and languishing. None of these things are objectively negative – these are feelings that are a part of the normal repertoire of human emotion – but they can become destructive, depending on how they are allowed to fester, and depending on how long they're allowed to control how we behave.

My experiences with mental health started years before the pandemic, as far back as 2011, and it comes to its conclusion in the recent present. Well, to as much of a conclusion as possible. After all, you can never eradicate all forms of loneliness, or make yourself flawless, or immunise yourself from mental health issues, but you can learn to manage these factors as part of a happy life. There will no doubt be future hurdles to jump over. The reason I am writing this now is because I am finally at a place where I can accept all parts of myself, the good and the bad, together as one. To some people I am the villain, and to some I am a great friend. Both versions of each and every one of us is true, and that's one of the hardest and most liberating things to accept.

Finally, this isn't meant to be a sad book. Some parts are sad, of course. But some parts of every life are sad. This isn't a book about making myself look good or to gain some sort of pity from you. There are parts of me discussed in this book that are monstrous. The darker sides of unaddressed flaws can be tough to look at directly and confidently. Yet, addressing them is paramount. Once you address the monsters in the dark, they become smaller and less dominating. The monsters under the bed become harmless dust bunnies once you look directly at them.

This book is about really looking at yourself, taking stock of the flawed image peering back, and learning to move forward, despite how hard the road ahead looks.

A man was given a gift one day. He opened the wrapping to find a small mirror. The note read: "You'd want to take a long hard look at yourself."

The Beginning

This story starts with an awful tragedy.

When I was 17 my best friend tried to kill himself. His name was Erbie. He passed away early on a Friday morning in January 2012. He died from blood clots after attempting to take his own life. He was in 6th Year at the time (The final year of Secondary School). After surviving his attempt, the blood clots became too severe and, while in hospital, he died as he got up to go to the bathroom. One day, everything was normal and then, suddenly, life became this nightmarish reality.

There are still a lot of unanswered questions about this time in my life. Questions about why Erbie felt he had to die. Questions regarding who was at fault and what had pushed him to the edge. Pointing the finger and trying to figure out what happened is too painful and it serves no good purpose. What happened cannot be unchanged and trying to unearth every detail only causes more hurt. I haven't always felt this way about it. There were times when I was consumed by anger, wanting to know exactly why he had to go. Eventually, I had to put the anger to rest though, because no matter what happened from then on, Erbie wasn't coming back. My best friend died by suicide at a very young age, and this is how the concept of mental health was introduced into my life. This is a scar that is sometimes, even now over ten years later, still an open wound. There were no such thing as mental health issues in my protected bubble until they came along and killed my best friend. It's a jarring realisation, realising how little mental health had ever been talked about before he died.

I still remember crying on the phone to my dad from the hospital when I found out. The tears made my face feel tight like saltwater always does. I was standing by a glass emergency exit door just off of the ICU in the Cork University Hospital, and I could see the spires of the city's churches like jagged teeth on the skyline. The sky was a tapestry of grey, and the tears fell from my eyes in a heavy downpour. My breath fogged the glass. Reality set in. My life changed forever.

This event mangled my mental landscape. All of a sudden, I was falling and unable to make any sense of why Erbie was gone. It changed who I thought I was, and who I would eventually become.

Erbie's death showed me the most horrific effect loneliness can have on a person. This is when I first learned that a person can literally die from feeling completely alone and isolated. When you feel so profoundly alone, you don't think you can come back from it. You don't think there is anyone who really cares about you. You don't believe there is anyone there that can make you feel safe. That's a very powerful and dangerous emotion, and it's one that affects a lot of us quietly. It's an emotion we fear, and therefore one we often do not acknowledge as it creeps up on us during the long and deadly night. And then one day, the feeling is too overbearing, and it takes full control.

The experience of losing a friend to suicide so young forced me to become an adult, possibly before I was ever meant to. People around me continued to enjoy the carefree aspects of adolescence, but for me, there was no longer any innocence. It was difficult to return to normal life and continue to care about things like parties and girls and sports teams, and all the other things that seem important to a teenage boy. Normal life became trivial as the harsh reality of death and suicide gripped me.

I remember one of my teacher's remarking on this months later, saying that I'd changed entirely in such a short space of time. Up until then I was still living carefree. There weren't many things in my life which were genuinely concerning, or that demanded high levels of stress and worry. It had all been manageable and relative to my day-to-day life. I worried about things like making basketball teams and getting enough X's in texts from the girl I liked. There was nothing which forced me to think about things in such real and harrowing ways. Death and the reality of mental illness were not common threads. I didn't even know about some of the things that people *could* worry about. I didn't know about anxiety and depression and loneliness and how lethal these things can be, or how common they really are.

Erbie's death shattered the glass ceiling and unveiled some of the harsher aspects of life. His death revealed some of the darkest experiences people have to deal with, and how some of these things can actually convince you to die if it gets bad enough. I couldn't see it at the time, and I didn't see it until years after, but the death of my closest friend had catastrophic effects on me. Effects that would become permanent fixtures rather than temporary setbacks. Of course, I knew back then that I was heartbroken and distraught, but I didn't consider how the effects of his death would ripple long into my 20s and no doubt beyond. I thought I'd grieve and move on like people usually do. A lot of people were able to do just that and get on with their lives. It wasn't like that for me. For whatever reason I couldn't move past it.

Suicide has a more sinister effect than death by other means, because a person we love opts out of life, and we can never say for sure exactly why they've done it. Forevermore, we will live wondering if we have left them down in some way, if there was more, we could have done. When a person kills themselves it's hard not to blame yourself to some degree for what happened. The terror of 'what if' keeps you up at night searching for answers that are impossible to find.

The last lucid interaction between Erbie and myself has haunted me because it happened on the same day he tried to kill himself, and for a very long time I questioned whether things would have turned out differently if I had chosen a different course of action that afternoon.

Erbie was in the year ahead of me in school. We both went to Douglas Com, the public secondary school in Douglas, Cork. Wednesdays were our half-days, and he found me after school – around 1PM – and asked if I wanted to get lunch. This wasn't unusual or out of the blue. It's something we often did before going our separate ways to complete schoolwork. At this time in 2012, you could get a dozen chicken wings from Tesco for around €1, to our delight, and we had been in the know for quite some time. That many chicken wings for so little money was like heaven for two young student athletes, in fairness. It had become a ritual of ours to tear down after school and gorge on these obscenely cheap chicken limbs. However, on this particular Wednesday afternoon I'd already made plans with lads from my own year – lads he wasn't really friends with – to head into town and meet some of the girls we knew who went to different schools. Not a big deal, I thought, we'd just hang out at the weekend as usual. So I declined Erbie's offer to lunch. We had basketball training the same evening and I didn't think anything of it. It was a normal interaction between the two of us, and one I didn't pay much mind to. There was no bad blood, we hugged it out and said we'd see each other at training.

That was the last time I saw him awake. He never showed up to training the same night, and there were no answers to my texts following the session. I assumed he was behind on schoolwork, as he so often was, so missing training wasn't totally unusual either. He may not have been allowed to come if he'd homework to do, and there was every chance his phone would be confiscated in a situation like that as well. Teenage things which happened to us all at some point.

None of that would have been out of the ordinary. Looking back, I wonder what the rest of his day looked and felt like. I can't even fathom how isolated he felt, and how terrified he was knowing his end was near. The loneliness he must have endured for so many long weeks isn't easy to think about, and it breaks my heart still to know he thought nobody cared.

The following morning – the Thursday – I was told he'd been taken to the hospital during the night. My Dad rang me during morning break to tell me. There was still optimism at that point, though. Although there would be a fallout and Erbie would need a lot of help to recover, he hadn't died. There was a sense of relief despite the harrowing circumstances. He'd been given a second chance.

I went up after school to see him. He was unconscious but alive. His lips were dry and flaky but other than this, he looked like he always did. I felt silly telling him I'd see him soon because he was unconscious, but I wanted him to hear my voice. I wanted to be able to talk to him, even if I couldn't say anything back. We left from the Emergency Ward shortly afterwards, and I went home worried, but confident that Erbie would pull through.

I was dead wrong.

He died in the early hours of Friday morning, as he got up to use the bathroom. There were blood clots everywhere.

Myself and Erbie's closest friends – Diarmuid, Mark, my brother Cillian – skipped morning classes to go up and see him. We got a card and filled it with inside jokes, things no one else would find remotely funny. There was an excited, and understandably nervous energy in the car. Although we were upset, we didn't even consider that Erbie could be dead based on my visit with him the previous afternoon. We simply didn't understand the situation though. Upon our arrival at the hospital, we were met by a nurse who looked the colour of old newspaper when we told her who we there to visit with. She led us to a room far away from the ICU, and this is where we found out, from Erbie's heartbroken mother, that our friend was never coming back.

After he died, I lingered on that last interaction we had after school, wondering if there was anything I could have done differently. Maybe if I had gone for lunch with him he would have opened up. Maybe he wouldn't have felt he needed to die if we could have just hung out that one stupid afternoon. It was easy to pin the blame to myself, because I had made the decision not to spend time with him. However, in a wider context, maybe if we'd learned about emotional awareness and emotional intelligence in school, he would have been able to open up, or I would have been able to spot that something was wrong. Maybe I had let Erbie down, but the education around mental health had let us all down long before then. There had never been any talks given to us about mental health or mental illness. In a typically Irish fashion, these things were left unsaid in the hope they would never come up. Our country's school system would rather sweep mental health under the carpet than have to have those uncomfortable conversations. But as we now know a decade later, these uncomfortable conversations save lives, and they are necessary to have.

Our last interaction will haunt me forever. It has been difficult to accept that there's nothing I could have done. It's been challenging to forgive myself for it. It's easy to look back now with the knowledge of what happened and wish I had done things differently, but I could never have seen this at the time. Some days the questions still arise, but I know now that there's nothing I could have done to help my friend on that Wednesday afternoon. However, at the time of his death, in those very raw early days, these thoughts -- the guilt and the what ifs -- consumed me.

This experience profoundly changed my understanding of mental health. It showed me how our wellbeing can be affected and how this struggle can often be a silent battle. People struggle all the time and hope that someone – anyone – will notice. Yet, people rarely notice because we are all so absorbed by our own lives. None of us can look out for anyone else if we're constantly focusing on ourselves.

My own mental health was damaged by my friend's suicide. In ways, the pain he felt was splintered and passed along to those of us who remained after him. It introduced me to intense grief, and opened up the floodgates for depression. Eventually, I became emotionally blunted and numb from it all, unable to register an emotion on any part of the spectrum. I hated that he didn't tell me he was suffering and felt for a long time felt that what he did was selfish. This was an ignorant and immature reaction but it's how I felt, and it would be disingenuous of me to leave it out or pretend like I felt otherwise. I hated myself, too. I hated myself for not being able to see it coming, for not being able to ask him what was going wrong. There was a lot of negative feelings surrounding that period of my life, and it took me a long time to forgive Erbie, and to forgive myself for what happened.

So, because none of us knew, and because he didn't know how to tell us, we lost him. We lost him because he felt utterly alone. He didn't think there was a way back from where he found himself, but there is always a way back. But when you're in that place the fog can be so heavy that you don't see the path. You don't believe the way back to safety exists anymore.

So we lost Erbie. We lost his smile, and his dirty laugh. We lost his love for plain scones and rap music. We lost his ability to make lay-ups with his left hand. His awkward looking jump-shot that somehow worked. We lost his jokes, his scowls. There would be no more quiet Erbie in the morning nor loud Erbie at the back of the bus. We lost all the little details that make a person, and we lost an entire lifetime of watching him grow.

When Erbie died I had a great support structure – I still do. I'm extremely lucky in this regard. I've never felt like I couldn't express myself or talk openly. That's a privilege I'm incredibly grateful to have and one I find myself thankful for today more than ever. But it's not one everybody is privy to, and I can only imagine how much worse I would have been if I didn't have such an understanding family and group of friends. Things might have turned out entirely differently then.

However, when we're in a low place all the support in the world will only do so much, and my world had been torn apart. Erbie and I were attached at the hip, and now there was only one of us left. When you're in a depressive spiral, the support around you is mostly ineffective if you are not voluntarily accepting of help. Voluntary action is required to get us out of low points, and it's the most difficult thing to do when you are there. There's a total lack of motivation because you can't see the point in any of it. So, although I had all the support I could ever need, I didn't care enough about me to voluntarily get the help I needed. I forced myself into loneliness and isolation because of how I was feeling.

I convinced my parents to let me get a tattoo of the words 'Live Through Me' not long after Erbie passed. I was only 17 so I needed their permission. In the end they let me, after much deliberation and negotiation. Any reasonable parent will have reservations about their child getting permanent ink forced into their skin. I felt it was a fitting tribute, allowing my brother to live through me because he could no longer do it for himself. He could live vicariously in a sense, even though I didn't think he was in a place where he could sense any of it. The symbol was more for me to remember him by than anything else.

It wasn't long before this symbolic gesture took on some pressure, though. In my mind I had to do enough living for two people now, and I only had enough life in me for one person. Not literally of course, but I suppose I just wanted to live as well as I could because he was no longer capable of it. But this put too much pressure on me – it made any mistakes or poor decisions twice as bad, and it split any good I did in two. I was desperate to have my friend back, for him to not be gone, and living as well as I could seemed like a good way to do that. I wanted to honour his life but I could never be him, the same way he could never have been me.

He had to live a fractioned life through me because we couldn't do enough to save him. I've never admitted that pressure to anyone because I always felt embarrassed about it – how a tattoo made me feel pressure to honour my friend – but that's how it felt for quite a long time. It's one thing to honour a loved one who has passed, it's another thing to take on the mantle of living for two people. I eventually stopped thinking I had to live for two people, and the pressure was relieved. The tattoo is old now and it's blotchy and scarred and hard to read, but I still see it every day and it reminds me of my friend, and of the good times we had, rather than the torturous memories of his death.

And so, this is where my journey with mental health began. I was immediately in the deep end, trying to make sense of a life taken too soon, and totally unaware of the tidal wave on the horizon.

Fallout

There's a strange sort of fraternity that grows from grieving a tragedy, which doesn't happen to the same degree with expected deaths. You and the ones who are suffering are bonded together by the trauma of it. Trauma then, is a strange sort of thing. Perhaps it's over cited in today's world, with every little flaw being chalked up to some unknowable trauma. Yet, the trauma created in the wake of such intimate tragedy is very real, and very prominent. You feel connected with others through your shared pain. It gives you a natural support mechanism to turn to without feeling uncomfortable about it. When the person across from you is just as fucked as you are, you don't feel as much hesitation to let it all out. You don't feel like what you'll say will make the other person feel awkward or distressed. You just say how you're feeling and it resonates. You can laugh and then cry and then say how sad you feel, and they will understand all of it. The shame aspect of admitting defeat diminishes. This is a unique aspect of grieving a suicide. Whereas the person who has gone did so because they felt totally alone, in the wake of their death you feel anything but alone. You feel like you and everyone around you has been shattered into a thousand pieces together, and so together you have to pick up whatever remains.

In the months after Erbie's death, there were plenty of moments to admit defeat. Crying myself to sleep was a regular thing. Bursting into tears randomly in school or at training happened plenty. Any gaps Erbie used to fill up were now pits of sadness as each gap highlighted his absence. My mother, God bless her, asked me often if I was feeling suicidal. I suppose it was only natural. There weren't any emotions registering with me. My mood was down, I wasn't sleeping and I was dissociating heavily. She couldn't bear the thought of me being gone, too. She was afraid that might become a reality, which was a reasonable concern to have. With everything going on, I can only imagine how scary that thought could have been. My parents had been close to Erbie as well. He was like a third son in the house. They told him this often – that he was a part of the Fleming family, and that he always had a place with us. His death was tearing us all apart. Hundreds of people grieving a man who thought he was alone is the definition of tragedy. As I said in the beginning, the experience of losing such a close friend at such a young age kickstarted my adult life. It set me on a course that I had no real control over.

Erbie's funeral was a kind of humanistic celebration, thankfully outside the grips of the church. I spoke, and spoke well I think, to what had to be over a thousand people about my friend. I didn't break down during that talk. I spoke about cherished memories and I spoke about what he meant to me. Other friends spoke, and sang, and recited poems, too.

In the days that followed there were a lot of hands shaken, and laughs had, and tears shed. I had to say goodbye to a dear friend, one who died for reasons I couldn't understand. Suicide, up until that point, was this vague tragedy that happened elsewhere, to other people completely removed from our world. It was outside the realms of possibility in our slice of reality. We had immunity to that sort of thing. I thought our lives would never be warped by such darkness.

The realisation that someone I knew so well, and was so close to could be fighting such a secret war without my knowledge was a terrifying thought. It took away my innocence. It took away the certainty I felt for the way things were. I realised that anyone could be feeling this way – alone and depressed – yet be hiding it away from the rest of the world. Suicide was no longer something that happened to other people in other places, it became a threat to everyone I knew. Depression doesn't care who or what you are, it can come silently and quickly during your darkest moments and it will try to convince you of some truly terrible lies.

As time moved forward, the months passing into years, I began to experience first-hand how mental health could deteriorate. I went through bouts of depression and fought with anxiety. I battled with long years of emotional numbness which harmed my relationships. These things still affect me at times. The lows come unexpectedly and rapidly, but the difference now is that I know how to deal with them a bit better than back then.

However, this knowledge only came after the experience, because there was no education in the secondary education system regarding mental health. Instead of gaining understanding through second-hand learning, many people in my generation and beyond have to learn about mental health issues by going through them. Our means of battling mental health problems are reactive rather than preventative, because a lot of misinformed people believe learning about such things increases the chances of these issues occurring. This is not true, and it's a harmful way to think. You don't develop other illnesses by becoming aware of them, that isn't how illness works.

Think about the impact of that. Many people can't identify the way they're feeling when new emotional states – like anxiety, like depression – roll in, because we don't have the words. Even in more recent years I've had people describe anxiety to me, yet have no knowledge that anxiety was what they were feeling. They had never heard a definition of anxiety and so they had come to believe that how they were thinking was just the way they were, and the way they had to be. They felt alone in how they felt because no one had told them how common anxiety really is. Many of us can intuit that something is wrong but we rarely understand what that something is. When you don't know what the problem is, you can begin to panic, and this can cause a lot of fear, and a lot of poor decision-making.

The point here is that, up until Erbie's death the notion of mental health was as alien to me as life from another planet. Looking back now, that seems incredibly irresponsible, to have mental health be a mystery to young people until the worst sort of tragedies strike, yet this is how the education system has historically approached mental health. Rather that prevent mental health related tragedies, our systems deal with the fallout of these tragedies in haphazard ways, after the fact.

On Becoming Numb

I had a girlfriend not long after Erbie died. She was lovely and nice and a firecracker. She didn't take shit from anyone, including me. I really liked her and she seemed to like me too, which seemed like madness on her account. She was there for me as much as a 17 year-old who'd never dealt with death could be, and I appreciated her for this.

Despite her understanding and best efforts, I felt overwhelmed juggling my grief and our relationship at the same time. I could barely hold myself up, let alone give another person the considerations one deserves in the early days of a relationship. It was too difficult to keep myself together enough to be able to support her in return. I remember finding myself in a back garden during a party one night not so long after Erbie was gone, crying onto one of my friend's shoulders. I hadn't been drinking, it was just a late night, lonely-in-a-crowd sort of realisation. Although months had passed there was still a lot of pain lingering in me and it came to a head that evening, up in a house in Grange one summer's evening. My friends didn't know what to do or say but they supported me, and they listened. I count myself lucky to have had people like that in my life at the time.

I felt stuck, and scared, and I didn't want to hurt anyone. I didn't think I could manage being there for someone as well as being there for myself. There were too many ways for me to feel like a burden. I ended our relationship a few days later without ever talking to her about why. I didn't explain myself. I didn't communicate. I didn't think there was a way I could grieve and still be a good boyfriend to her, but I never told her why I was ending things. I was young, and very stupid, and if I'd been able to communicate, then I have no doubt things would have been far different. It got sloppy after that because we got back together briefly, before I ended it again in quick succession. I was all over the place and I was beginning to hurt people as I fell apart. Although I didn't want to hurt anyone, I ended up doing exactly this.

That was the last real relationship I've been in, and I was only 17 then. I've avoided admitting this to myself for the entirety of my adult life because it feels embarrassing to admit that a man on the edge of his late twenties has never been in a long-term adult relationship, but it's true. I've regularly been seeing people and dating, but I've never allowed myself to become vulnerable enough to be in a relationship since Erbie died. And there are reasons for this which I have denied to myself for close to ten years. Although, I've made huge strides mentally since, there have clearly been some underlying problems allowed to exist unresolved. I've neglected relationships in the past to work on myself, while still trying to engage in romantic endeavours. I was essentially trying to swim with heavy weights pulling me under the water. You can't choose to not be in a relationship yet constantly seek them out. You can't know you're not in the right place emotionally yet lead people on without explaining yourself. That isn't fair to anyone. I needed to heal so that I could be ready for a functioning relationship but I also didn't want to be alone, and this led to a string of short-lived relationships, usually ending because I needed to run from the vulnerability. This is a part of my mental self which I purposefully ignored because it was too painful to address. I didn't want to admit that I had this big, gaping hole in who I was, but denying that it existed only made the hole bigger, and the problem worse.

The fallout from my friend's death damaged my ability to feel, express, and understand emotion. I liken it to a circuit board getting too much electrical input – eventually it burns out and can't output anything at all. This is when a blackout happens. There were so many powerful emotions passing through me that I blew a fuse and could no longer handle the input. After weeks and months of sadness laid on thick, I was suddenly numb to everything. I no longer felt sad. I felt indifferent. Nothing mattered anymore. There was no joy either. It was just a consistent nothingness. I was indifferent to things going on around me and found myself going through the motions in order to hide the truth of the situation. As the years dripped passed, this numbness eased, but it never truly left. I've had to work on expressing emotion. I don't always get it right. It can be hard knowing people are expecting an emotional reaction yet feeling nothing. You feel like you're letting them down in some way, like you're not giving them what they deserve.

Over time, the problem morphed from not being able to feel anything to not being able to express a feeling. Sometimes I feel something but the manifestation of it isn't very intense. It feels like trying to understand someone underwater – yes, I know I am feeling something but it is sometimes quite difficult to know what it is because it's so feint. I can hear the voice shouting but I couldn't tell you at all what it might be saying. This could be due to long periods of feeling nothing, but it resulted in not being sure what to do when I know I should be feeling something but can't feel a thing. Writing has helped that. Although sometimes I can't express my feelings in person, it's easier for me to articulate the emotions in the written word. That's why writing is therapeutic for me, and it's why I'll always do it even if no one is reading. I can find ways to express myself in writing that I've always struggled to do in real time.

That said, I still struggle with emotional numbness and an inability to express myself from time to time, but I've learned to work on it and be patient with myself. I've become aware of an issue I had been denying to myself for years, and now I actively work on it. This feels like progress. But these things rarely fix themselves overnight. The awareness of our flaws is an important foundation on which to rebuild ourselves.

It was unknown to me for some time, but this inability to express or accept emotion in the context of a relationship is called *emotional unavailability*. It happens to people for an array of different reasons. For me, becoming attached to people felt daunting and it scared me, so my work around was to limit how attached I could become to people, things, accomplishments. This meant I never got too high, or too low, in public or in private. I've always just been on an even keel which is obviously helpful in a lot of situations. I rarely lose my temper, for example. Bad news doesn't often upset me because I don't take these matters personally, because there's no emotion attached to them for me. This unattachment clearly has its benefits, but it's also a mindset synonymous with being alone. When you don't attach or feel intense emotions people assume you don't care enough and walk away.

If you met me you wouldn't describe me as excitable, or enthusiastic. It sometimes seems like things don't phase me, or that I don't care about things I ought to care about. People often joke about how unenthusiastic my voice sounds. However, I do get enthusiastic and care about many things, historically I just haven't been good at showing this. I do feel emotions I just often struggle to express them. There was a layer of numbness that surrounded me emotionally for some years and so it sometimes takes a lot more for me to feel a visceral emotion than it would take for other people. I need a lot more fuel to get the same fire going.

This was caused by two things. The first, as we have discussed, was the trauma of losing my friend to suicide. The second reason I became emotionally unavailable was because I failed to resolve something which happened before Erbie passed. My then girlfriend cheated on me multiple times, and betrayed my trust. This was a girl I was head over heels for and I ended up getting my heart shattered.

I'd known in my gut that something was wrong but I ignored it because of how I felt about her. I didn't want to believe what I knew instinctively to be true because it meant the end of what we had. This mistake in judgement ended up causing devastation. At that young age, knowing that I was punching out of my league, I was clingy and overbearing. It didn't help the situation, and it would have made sense if she had flat out dumped my ass, but it still didn't justify cheating and hurting me to that degree.

From this, I learned a very maladaptive defence mechanism -- that I should never feel so much for someone again, so as to avoid that level of hurt. Every other person was ruled out because of the actions of one very careless person. But the overcorrection meant that I would go on to hurt other people. I would never settle down. I would see multiple people at once. I would never become vulnerable with anyone. Imagine if we overcorrected this much in other aspects of our lives. Never wearing shoes again because a specific pair gave you blisters. Never using soap again because you got some in your eyes that one time. It makes little sense to overcorrect in this way but we often do it, and it usually causes us more harm than anything else. But it *feels* right. It felt like I was protecting myself, but I was really denying myself the chance to move on.

I didn't resolve this trust issue for years, and it caused me to become closed off from opening up to another relationship. I'm still working on that. I'm still learning to open myself up to people, to let them in, and let myself be vulnerable to the possibility of being hurt again. It has to be done, but it's always been difficult for me. I have never sincerely let my guard down, and this has resulted in many potential relationships fizzling out because I have been reluctant to trust anyone. I have been reluctant to risk feeling that level of pain again, and this is why, at 27 years old there isn't anyone I could reasonably say I've had a long-term and serious relationship with.

Due to these event, and due to my inability to resolve the issues they caused, I have for quite some time, had difficulty in expressing or even feeling emotions. There have been countless situations where, although I can't feel the emotions, I have known which emotions were expected of me. The problem here isn't so much an empathy problem, it's an error in being able to feel the emotion that I ought to be feeling. I know what happiness and sadness and anger look and feel like, but I only ever felt very faint versions of them.

Therefore, because I understood what the appropriate emotional response would be in a given situation, I was able to exaggerate the fleeting things I did feel. I became an emotional chameleon, changing my colours based on the context I found myself in. Because I knew what emotions would be appropriate, I was able to pretend to be happy or excited or upset or whatever it may have been. I'd know that people would expect me to be happy over an achievement so I'd perform this for them. It is ultimately strange for people when they ask me if I'm delighted and appear to be feeling nothing. You'd find it hard to believe an unsmiling face is delighted about whatever just happened. I feigned emotion to make everyone else comfortable because I knew that if the people around me saw that I wasn't feeling anything that this could be concerning or distressing. The last thing I wanted was for people to realise that I wasn't able to express my emotions. There has been a real fear of being 'found out' for this because in my mind it meant that I'd be classified as broken.

In this way, I could feel enough empathy to understand how others were feeling, I just couldn't jump start the emotions within myself. They were feint sensations. Eventually, I had enough of the emotion to know exactly which one I was meant to feel, and then all I had to do was exaggerate it to the desired level. It can be quite strange knowing that all the conditions are in place to feel happiness yet feel nothing. It's not that I was overly sad, I literally felt nothing at all. The mind can be a weird place when this happens, especially when the people around you are effortlessly feeling and expressing emotions all over the place. It feels like you're the last person on Earth without an internet connection.

In the past few months and years, I've become more aware of this problem. It has been leading me away from the possibility of happiness, and I was content to let this happen, because I didn't think happiness was something I deserved. From my perspective, if emotions weren't something I could feel and express then there was a good reason for that. I framed this lack of ability as the will of the universe rather than something that can and should be worked on. I gave myself the excuse of it being unfixable because the work ahead was too big of a mountain to deal with. It was a cop out, and only recently have I begun to genuinely work on this stunted emotional issue because my life satisfaction got so low. Not being able to reciprocate emotionally has been a challenge in every relationship I've had, and I'm tired of it resulting in me being alone.

These days, I force myself to label how I'm feeling, no matter what the feeling is or how little I feel. I'll tell people if I'm happy or if I'm anxious or if I'm feeling sad. Saying the words out loud is helpful; it allows me to identify exactly what's happening rather than letting it sink under the more rational and passive part of my personality. Instead, I now actively engage with my emotions so that I can feel them more strongly. This means allowing myself longer moments of happiness or sadness or anxiousness or excitement when they percolate through. It feels like I'm retraining my limbic system. I spent so many years not feeling much of anything that for the last number of months and years I have had to purposefully feel things. I have to choose to feel things if I am to feel them at a level strong enough for genuine and authentic expression. If I don't, then it's all theatre to make people, including myself, feel more comfortable.

And this choosing, this mindful emotional awareness, is something that has worked, that is working, and these days I can feel things vividly without any guilt for having felt them. Not always, but definitely more often than ever before. I no longer feel embarrassed for getting excited, or ashamed for feeling sad. I welcome everything now, because feeling things is a sure sign that we are alive. I challenge you to stop and be aware the next time you are upset or anxious or crying and, even though the feeling is negative, take stock of how alive you feel. Understand that these experiences are what life is, and that they should be embraced. We are emotional beings, and so feeling an emotion is to be alive.

It is less likely now that I will brush over an emotion. I feel things more vividly because I allow myself to. For years I stopped giving myself permission to feel things because I thought that I couldn't be hurt if I couldn't feel emotions. Although it may true that it stopped me from being hurt from the outside, it caused a lot of problems to arise from the inside. I unintentionally caused a lot of damage to my emotional landscape in order to protect myself from potential devastation.

Sometimes, I still 'put on' the emotions, but more often, I allow myself to feel whatever way I'm feeling, and try and understand that there are no 'correct' ways to feel about anything. We feel one way for a while and then we stop and feel another way. Feelings are like trains coming and going from the station. Emotions come and go, and I neither try to deny them to myself nor force them to stay longer than they should stay. Rather than avoiding feeling things like I used to, I seek out emotions when they're appropriate, and I think my mental health, relationships, and general understanding of myself has improved tremendously for it.

Man Feelings

The year after Erbie's death I sat the Leaving Cert and had to decide what I wanted to do with the rest of my life. I always performed well in school, but I had no idea what I wanted to do in any real sense. There was never a clear path forward for me, no career that jumped out trying to gain my attention. I was jealous of my brother and other friends who seemed to have been born with this knowledge. It was as obvious to them as the nose on my face what their lives would subsequently look like. I had no clue but felt I had to pretend as if I did. I couldn't let people know I was unsure of myself. That type of information getting leaked could lead to momentary mortification which would be too much to handle altogether. It's bizarre that we normalise the idea that an 18 year-old should know what they want to do for the next 40 years of their life at such a young age. You're a weirdo if you don't know. You're off the beaten track if college isn't the clear next step for you. It has become the norm for 18 ear-olds to make life changing decisions under incredible pressure, rather than taking more time to mature and find out what they're really passionate about. For some terrible reason, it's more important that we are sprinting in any direction than it is to be walking in the correct one.

The baptism of fire I had with mental health and my fixation on the obliterating effects poor mental health can have pushed me towards psychology. Having done exam religion for my Leaving Cert, I had already grown quite fond of philosophy. (I only sat religion so I wouldn't have to count Irish and French in my points. These were my worst subjects, so tactical religion was the way forward). I wanted to learn more about the mind so that I could protect myself from the trials that Erbie faced, plus help others to work through their own mental health issues more effectively in time, so that nobody else would have to take their own life. Applied Psychology in UCC became my number one choice and I didn't think much more about it. I became fascinated with cognition, memory, and what could go wrong in people's brains to cause them to fall into poor mental health.

I had no clear idea as to what had caused Erbie to get to such a dark place. Well, I did have some idea, but I didn't know for certain. He never spoke to me in any real sense about his demons. I knew that he was struggling in school, mainly due to lack of interest rather than lack of ability, which is common. How many teenagers don't like school though? Quite a lot, so none of that was necessarily unusual. It wasn't a situation you'd ever consider abnormal if you were looking in from the outside. When Erbie was with us, he was laughing and full of life and cracking jokes and chasing women – he did all of the things most teenagers do.

He hadn't any real time for talking about feelings. None of us really did at the time, I suppose. Feelings were best addressed privately, and in an all-boys school, any sign of emotion was a sign of weakness. I know now that this is a big part of the problem. It was years after his death before I understood how little men really talk about how they're feeling, and how much of an issue this is. The society we live in has always positioned men as resilient, unemotional, silent beings. It's the way men 'should be.' This is neither true nor realistic. Men account for more than three quarters of all suicides. These days, we're encouraged to speak up which is good, but it's not enough.

I often notice that men are told that the way they feel is wrong. That they are feeling the wrong ways about things. In a progressive society that screams 'All feelings are valid' it seems tone deaf to suggest that men are wrong for feeling certain ways. You can't tell a person to talk while at the same time demand that they are quiet. Dealing with masculine mental health problems is different to dealing with feminine ones. Each gender reacts differently to situations – with men tending to try and move past an issue, and women tending to talk about them more openly. The solution for men's mental health issues isn't to eradicate masculinity, nor is the solution to use feminine solutions to address specifically masculine problems, and vice versa. The solution lies in finding ways for men to deal with their issues in ways that are most effective for them, on an individual basis. The same goes for the issues faced by women. There is no one size fits all solution to these issues, and it shouldn't be suggested that there is. Our culture in Ireland tends to believe that the ways in which men deal with their emotions is wrong, but this only further propagates the stigma around men feeling things at all. There is an ethos of 'masculinity is bad' and 'femininity is good' slowly taking over our world, and this is a very counter-productive way to view it. There is no nuance and therefore, no attempt to understand what's really going on. It not only teaches young women to hate men, but it also teaches young men that their very existence is somehow problematic.

In the years that followed, I went to college and studied psychology. College was an incredibly happy time for me in many ways. I was able to put the trauma of those last years in school behind me. I met some people who became friends, friends who have stayed in my life ever since. I flourished at times. I played basketball for the university team, I went to parties, I stayed out all night. I lived a life that felt normal. For a while, I forgot about my unresolved mental health issues, which floated below the surface like debris under the ice of frozen lakes.

However, it was also a very low time for me. In college I realised the extent of my depression, and how emotionally blunted Erbie's death had made me. I realised that I hadn't gotten over his death at all, I'd merely learned to live with the demons, as they festered in the back of my mind.

So there I was, emotionally scarred and numb, unsure of the road ahead. I didn't even know it at the time, but this numbness would affect every relationship in my life.

Breaking Point

In college you learn that the session comes before the learning, but you're never to admit this out loud to a 'real' adult. If parents knew the true extent to which studies are left out in the rain, they would not pay the high price to send their beloved children to university. This is an unspoken truth known only by those who have attended college. College is a more of a three-to-four year bender with some lectures sprinkled throughout than it is a full-time education with the occasional night out. If you're a parent of a student and you're reading this, I'm only joking, of course.

For those of you uninitiated, Raise & Give week (also known by the much cooler and easier to say, Rag Week) is a five day event in the second semester of a given college year, which aims to raise much needed funds for some very deserving charities. College campuses become home to food trucks and stage hypnotists and poster dispensaries and guest lecturers and many, many student led events. It is a time to showcase the culture of university life, and it exemplifies what it means to attend university. The campus is alive and thriving and feels as much like an American campus you'd see in the movies as Ireland can muster. It can be a very wholesome time and is a great week to be hyper involved in any of the available university societies.

However, Rag Week is also synonymous with a five-day balls-to-the-wall drinking session for students, each night taking on a different designated bar or club, and each day spent trying to fend off hangovers, drinking more than is ever required of anyone, and ignoring any niggling feeling that some college work should at least be attempted. Underneath the veil of raising money for charity, Rag Week is secretly devoted to binge drinking and partying. The fundraising is unfortunately secondary in this marathon of debauchery. Both students and lecturers know scheduled classes during this week are just a formality, and often they are cancelled or postponed. Often, a lecturer will be surprised and/or disappointed to find you showing up to class during Rag Week, as this means you have now forced them to do a job they otherwise would have had a break from. This week is an unofficial hiatus from student life across all levels of the college and it is simultaneously welcomed and protested against with equal amounts of vigour.

Rag Week is the ultimate party-endurance event, with the primary focus being to inflict optimal damage upon young livers. It's safe to say that Rag week is any college student's event of the year. It's a tribute to everything it means to be in college; partying, drink, drugs, sex and a complete avoidance of any of the actual reasons for enrolling to begin with. Lack of responsibility is king in this empire.

It's a sort of paradise for most students.

I enjoyed this week of every year as much as anyone. However, I was wired a little differently to my contemporaries. Not in any sort of *'I'm better than you'* way, more so in the way that I was too anxious to fully immerse myself in the week away from college work. The thought of falling behind was too much for me, and I still found myself doing at least a small amount of work every day to mitigate the guilt of partying at night. Back then, I wasn't really affected by hangovers, and so being productive the day after the night before was on the cards.

I still participated in the festivities as much as I could. I enjoy a rambunctious session when I'm on form, although as the years go on the hangovers from such sessions make them less and less worthwhile. These days recovering from self-poisoning can last anywhere from 1-3 days, and so the reason for drinking needs to be worthwhile. But back then, any reason was a good enough reason to land onto a gaff with 8 cans without a need to be anywhere else. Suckling at the metallic end of silver-bullets with friends is one of the purest forms of hedonism a young person can partake in. Alcohol is part and parcel for life in Ireland in general, let alone in the microcosm of university life. We tend to use any event as an excuse to get pissed on our little island. I'm not saying our relationship with alcohol as a people is healthy – far from it – but it is a huge part of the culture, for better or for worse. So college for me was the same as it is for most other students. It was a time to drink as much as possible without letting it ruin my academic career, and this was indeed a fine balance to strike.

That being said, I never went out every single night of Rag Week. During my time in UCC, I experienced three of these weeks, and whilst some of my friends took Rag Week seriously for the marathon event that it is, I had gut feelings that my mind couldn't hack that sort of intensity. I had never been one for endurance sports and I knew I didn't have the stamina to maintain a week of drinking, whilst also working part-time and trying to keep up with college work. I was also heavily involved in basketball back then and there was virtually no way I could ever allow myself to skip a training session. I attended as many lectures as possible during these weeks, went to training and/or the gym, and made sure I was on top of whatever work was due while also doing what I could to make it out for as many nights as possible. Older readers will call this sensible and mature, younger readers will call this dry and sad. I'm somewhere in between both those conclusions myself. The real reason I did these things wasn't some heightened level of discipline either – it was because of the anxiety that comes with not doing the things I felt I ought to be doing. I knew I'd feel a gut-altering guilt if I skipped out on any of my usual commitments just to drink, and so for me the partying could only be done once all other responsibilities were catered for. A college student might say I had my priorities wrong, and there's a good chance they'd be correct.

This is something I refer to as productivity guilt, or anxiety. (More on this later). Productivity guilt is that restlessness, that inability to relax or enjoy yourself because you know there is something you *ought* to be doing. You can't put down the tools until the job is done. There is absolutely no chance that you can truly enjoy yourself if there is some work left. It feels like you have no entitlement to downtime. You've felt it at some stage undoubtedly – everyone has. The problem for me is that I feel this non-stop, all day, every day. Some days it's very loud and unrelenting, other days it's quiet and ignorable.

Up until my second year of college I had never done any drugs apart from taking brief tokes from an infrequent joint from time to time (And also alcohol, which is definitely one of the worst drugs but isn't really considered one for some reason). Weed was something I could take or leave and it never got to a point where I learned to roll my own joints because the investment wasn't worth the return. Smoking marijuana is something I have done semi-often but isn't 'drug use' in my eyes. It never felt like a drug in a real sense because it didn't do the mind-altering things that I was led to believe drugs did. Weed makes movies more entertaining and it makes food taste better, but it's unlikely to make inanimate objects talk, or allow you to speak to God in some other dimension. Aside from those rare nights of THC-induced sleepiness, I stuck to my cans of beer and pints and I was happy out, destroying my body in ways deemed acceptable by wider society. My health – both mental and physical – probably would have been better served if I only smoked weed and left the drink off, but this wasn't the route that was normalised by civilisation, and so it wasn't the route I took.

Alcohol had always been a part of my university experience, and was inescapable in a lot of ways. I drank when I wanted to, and I didn't drink when I didn't want to. However, in the second year of my undergrad, ecstasy took my year group by storm. Everyone in my immediate social circles suddenly seemed to be doing the party drug. It came out of nowhere and dominated the nightlife. Each night out was accompanied by these tiny pills that cause jaws to swing and pupils to dilate to the size of two euro coins. Drink on its own was suddenly no longer enough to enjoy oneself. Pre-town parties became the scenes you'd see in those corny anti-drug ads from the early 2000s. Little pills were passed between concealed palms, or were placed intimately onto tongues in open mouths. There was a giddy energy that rang a little shady, too. It felt sinister, but it also felt rebellious, like the people who did the drug were drawing outside of the lines on purpose and saying a big 'Fuck you' to anyone who gave out about it. They were living outside of the rules our parents had laid down, and it was tantalising it its way.

Ecstasy took my peers to a higher level of party-consciousness and it began to feel like the inner circle had only one way in. They talked more about energy and less about being fucked. They connected dots where no dots had been connected before. Their pupils enlarged and they appeared out of the darkness of nightclubs like low-budget aliens looking for a good time rather than people to abduct. Jaws swung as lose as grips on reality. To me, it felt like I was watching them from the shallows whilst they did crazy somersaults into the deep end of the pool from a diving board I was too afraid to climb up to.

It's difficult to explain how much of a barrier not being on a certain substance put up during those college nights out. Suddenly you're watching your friends enjoy the rollercoaster instead of being on it with them. Whereas before there was a commonality, for the most part, by drinking together shamelessly, now there was a jumping-off point. There was a distinct yet unspoken split in the group between those who did the drug and those who did not.

Back then, I felt guilty about even doing benign things like staying out late or not coming home at all, so the idea of choosing to do an illegal substance was initially a non-runner. I felt bad for even considering it. I had a very rigid notion of right and wrong, not understanding that morality could be context-dependent. I never questioned my beliefs, or whether they could be misled. I was altogether too certain that behaving in a certain way was bad and that I'd also be bad if I participated. This is a terribly narrow way to consider moral behaviour, but it's important to note here, because it is altogether too easy and too common for us to be filled with gratuitous certainty that how we think now is absolutely and irreversibly correct, across all contexts. There's an arrogance to that which is uniquely human. I believed using drugs in all contexts was bad (despite my use of 'approved' drugs) and therefore I believed that taking any drug would suddenly and definitively make me a bad person.

Eventually however, taking ecstasy felt like a requirement for acceptance. If you didn't ride this wave then you were benched, no longer part of the tight-knit circle. What I'm trying to say is drugs gatekeep having the craic. And when you want to have the craic, but don't seem to be having the same amount of craic as the people around you, you'll eventually do anything to be able to join in on said craic, especially if you begin to feel isolated. My stance on drug use began to shift based on the lack of craic I was having, and using ecstasy as a means of joining the group suddenly became far more enticing. I began to rationalise it in my head, ignoring my own moral qualms.

I'd never been one for peer pressure's allure. When it comes to potentially controversial behaviour, or things that could land one in trouble, I've always acted out of choice rather than pressure from external forces, like friends or people I wanted to impress. Generally, when it comes to acting right now in this moment, I just do what feels right for me. However, during Rag Week of second year, I suddenly felt more outside of the friend group and alone than ever. I wanted to be in. I felt that being in the group would make me feel better and would stop me from feeling left out. I wanted to be seen and to be involved. Instead of addressing why I felt this way inside, I externalised the solution. I needed the validation of others during those years because, unbeknownst to myself, I wasn't very happy with who I was. Entry into the upper echelons of my social group was enticing and I wanted it. I wanted other people to like me in order to feel good about myself. Luckily for me, I knew the price of admission, so I decided to pay.

I remember it so well because it ended so badly. We were in one of the girls' houses not far from College Road pre-drinking before heading out for the Tuesday night of Rag Week – arguably the biggest night of the week. Those streets around the university were filled with open front doors, blaring music, and drunken students every few steps. Real adults, if they were unlucky enough to live in that area, kept their doors closed and their curtains drawn. Although that week is heaven for students, it is living hell for anyone else in proximity. The street my friends lived on was a hill, dotted with constantly full wheely-bins, and lined on either side with Toyota Yaris' and Volkswagen Golfs. If college accommodation had a scent, it was the low hum of vomit and stale cider that whipped up from those roads in the rain.

What had become the standard procedure for our nights out initiated around 8PM. We'd arrive up – that is, the lad-folk of the college crew - with cans and small bottles of vodka tucked into back pockets. The girls were more than likely upstairs getting ready, hurling abuse at us for being too early as always, even though we were on time. One of the lads filled the quiet living room with music and the festivities began to the sound of cracking cans of cheap beer filling the small space. The pageantry of it all was subtle but intoxicating.

The pills were present quietly as always -- in the sleight of hand as they passed around the room filled with a mixture of users and non-users. The music drummed on, and we all shouted over it so that we could be heard and so that we could hear. I told one of the usual partakers, a close friend of mine, that I might want to board the train that evening. I felt awkward as the alien words fell from my lips. The excitement from him, and then later from the rest of them, was encouraging in fairness, and that only fuelled my desire to take the drug. They treated me as if I'd finally found my way into a secret room. I was no longer an observer on the outside – I was 'in' and it made me feel good.

I was handed an insignificant blue pill which had a tiny imprint of a ghost on it, and was told to take it whenever I wanted. I couldn't even feel the weight of it in my palm and wondered about what exactly it was in that microscopic tablet that would soon cause me to see behind the curtain. The details of exactly how I would know when the drugs were working were vague – they simply told me I'd definitely know when it happened, and if I was unsure then it had not happened yet. I drank a few more cans to build up some extra courage and slipped out into the empty kitchen away from the rest of the group. Once alone, I took the pill out of my jeans pocket for a look.

This tiny thing in my palm was allegedly going to make my night a whole lot better. It was about the size of an antihistamine. Ignoring the alarm bells going off in my head, I placed it on my tongue like a Communion wafer, and washed it down with whatever beer I was drinking. As I felt it disappear down my throat the way morning vitamin tablets do, I couldn't help but feel that I had just made a very bad decision. I could feel it prominently in my gut, and the feeling washed over me like rain. This wasn't a very *me* thing to do, nor was it something that I would ever have given thought to in the past, and I knew it. I felt guilty instantly. The regret manifested. I tried to shake the thought from my mind as I returned to the party and sipped feverishly at my beer. The excitement of the others for me to join in was palpable, and I kept telling myself I was making a big deal over nothing, which I probably was. Unfortunately, as I soon came to learn, the instinct of your gut is rarely wrong, and it's hard to rationalise away a bad feeling. The regret I felt would become the baseline for the experience I was about to have.

Coming up, as it's known, is a strange experience. There's no slow burn to madness as there is with drinking, nor is there the calm melting effect which comes with getting high. It's far more invasive and immediate and intense. It changes how you feel within a moment with no warning of its beginning. At least with drinking you can understand how aggressive the inebriation is going to be, based on how much more alcohol you consume. Coming up feels like a fire has been lit under the conscious part of your brain, but without the pain associated with fire. The air around you begins to vibrate. Your sense of 'self' rises about 12 inches above your head, so it feels like your brain has gotten bigger. You feel as though you're looking down on yourself from above, while simultaneously being more inside of your skull than you have ever been before. Your skin tingles with a sort of euphoric electricity and everything is much louder. The input is massive. Every sensation is more vibrant and interesting and mind-blowing. You will want to talk for fucking hours – and you will.

This initial feeling lasted about 30 seconds for me before it was replaced with the very real fear of getting arrested and thus, nabbed for being high as a kite. I came up as we got out of the taxi in town, the taxi which was forced to stop by swarming Gardaí. As my pupils dilated and I began to lose subtle control of my jaw, we turned a corner into absolute chaos. There were Gardaí everywhere for some reason. Bright neon-clad keepers of the law were all around us. There was a checkpoint, and it being the week it was meant there was mayhem. It's the busiest week in the city centre during the college year without a doubt. Gardaí (the Irish police force) were stopping cars and taxis before they reached the epicentre of the session, making eager students walk the remaining hundred metres or so to their destinations in order to alleviate congestion.

Our taxi came to a halt and we scrambled out from the backseat, hoping to walk the rest of the way. By then I was freaking out because I was higher than I'd ever been from anything and I was certain the pesky Gardaí would know we were on drugs, and that I would then be arrested for being on the drugs and that this would result in my life being over forever. I avoided eye contact as much as anyone has ever avoided eye contact. I was being slightly dramatic, but I also wasn't 100% sure if I could remember how to walk.

Luckily for me – now resembling a pound-shop ET – there was too much going on for the Gardaí to take any notice of our neat party, and they shepherded us over the bridge and down into Hanover

Street without any suspicions that we were out of our minds. I let out a long sigh of relief as electric energy pulsated through my arms and down my legs into my feet. We walked the short distance to Hanover, where most of the clubs were at the time. This was where the entirety of students were heading for, like pilgrims to the Promised Land.

When we turned the corner onto the street, I was absolutely blown asunder by how many people were jammed in between the buildings. I'd never seen so many people crammed onto that laneway. In my mind, it seemed like everyone who currently existed in Cork was on this one narrow street. It seemed completely impossible to me that there could be so many people. It was jam packed and it very quickly began to make me feel trapped and uncomfortable. Never having been one for the fear of crowds, there was a sudden rush of panic as I fixated on just how many people were around me.

I'd never in my life taken notice of how many people were in any given place before, but with the effects of MDMA in my blood, it was all I could think of, and all I could focus on. There was nothing else I could see other than the sheer volume of drunken students. We began to navigate through them like a small boat on a stormy sea and I could feel people pressed up against me from all angles. Sweaty, intoxicated students all making their way into the night. All living out their own complex storylines that were no doubt equally as dumbfounding as mine. The sense of sonder was prolific. Elbows jabbed and foul breath attacked my nostrils. I stuck close to whoever was walking in front and hoped I wouldn't get lost in the mayhem. I could hear lads hollering after girls and young ones shouting at their friends to hold on a second longer. There was laughter and screaming and excitement on the air. You could almost hear the hum of energy emanating from the crowd. There were beer cans flying and glasses breaking, and so much noise and too many people. I felt like I was drowning in this sea of drunken students. I was fucking terrified.

We eventually found our way into a queue against a wall for one of the night clubs, and my heart was doing ninety. It felt like I might soon collapse, or vomit at the very least. I couldn't stop moving – I bounced from one foot to the other and kept my hands occupied with my keys inside my pockets – and found myself fixating on the windows of the building opposite. I thought that if I could just keep counting the windows then maybe I'd forget about all the people, and in this way, I could calm myself down. I'd never looked upwards in this section of the city before, and found that there were far more windows than I would have predicted. My breathing was out of control now and it felt like my lungs were going to burst out of my chest. I was fidgeting my hands and trying to appear normal and in control, as my friends geared up to give their IDs to the bouncer.

I'd never felt such fear and I couldn't stop it. The drugs had taken over and I had no control over anything. I'd gone past the point of rationalising myself into calmness. That tiny insignificant pill made me aware of how many people there were in the street, and my mind told me it was entirely reasonable that I should panic over this fact. I was moving and breathing heavily, and my heart was pounding, and I just stared at the fucking windows and counted them without ever actually keeping count, and none of it helped. The situation I found myself in didn't equate to the euphoria I was promised. I wondered how long I'd have to manage this ordeal, hoping it wouldn't last longer than a few minutes.

It must have been obvious something was wrong because my friend, the one who had given me the pill in the first place, turned and asked if I wanted to leave, to which I immediately agreed to. There was thick, cold sweat layering my forehead now and I was sure I'd gone pale as a ghost based on the way he was looking at me – he was extremely high, but was still openly concerned. Even if I'd decided to stay and tough it out, there was no chance of getting in anywhere with the condition I was in. I was very obviously on drugs and not handling it all that well. Any bouncer would have taken one look at me and guided me immediately out of line and towards the nearest late-night café.

Myself and two of the lads (all three of us high on MDMA) left Hanover Street to the dismay of our friends, and went back to one of the houses. I remember feeling very grateful that they'd sacrificed their night out to take care of me. Once there, I began to calm down. Things were much more manageable once we landed onto a familiar location. Without the crowds and noise and claustrophobia inducing conditions, I felt less on edge and could begin to feel the more subtle hints of the ecstasy's seduction. Since we were on MDMA there was absolutely no chance of sleep anytime soon. Although we'd opted out of the nightclub, we still had to get through the 6-8 hours we'd promised to the party drug. We were wired and ready for a lot of conversation. It would be a late one regardless of whether I chose to enjoy it or not. Luckily, once it was just us three in a safer and quieter environment, I began to appreciate the effects of the drug and began to feel good about what was going on.

We had some profound conversations about nothing I can remember, which were undoubtedly not very profound at all. I'm sure we believed we'd solved all the problems faced by the world. We also sang openly and listened to music, hearing old tunes through fresh ears. Our jaws swung from ear to ear, and we rattled like teeth from the surging adrenaline. There was no stone left unturned that night. Eventually, after hours of non-stop talking, we went to sleep in the late hours of the morning as the sunlight began to drift through the curtains.

It was a significant night for me, and one that I'd recall over and over again throughout the following years. Later, I'd recount to friends and strangers, the first time I tried ecstasy and the panic attack I endured as a result. Significant nights don't always have to be good memories, they just have to bring you to a place where you unlock a new truth about who you are, and who you think you should be. Lessons like these don't generally come in the form of positive outcomes. Which is why it is important to be aware that, even if things seem terrible right now, you are at least gaining invaluable experience and understanding, which makes bad experiences worthwhile in the long run.

That all went down on the Tuesday night of Rag Week in 2015. It's etched into my memory like a tattoo. I was at the peak of my denial. The morning after I could no longer ignore the fact that I was in a bad place. It had all come to a head. I'd tried a real drug for the first time, not because I wanted to, but because I felt I had to. It was the first time I had a full blown panic attack, and the first time I was forced to admit something hadn't been right for quite some time. I had never even considered drug use up until that point. I don't think there's anything wrong with using them, but that night I didn't choose to use them for the right reasons. I had chosen to use them because I felt left out, because I wanted to be liked. And it's important to ask myself why that is? Why all of a sudden did I care about being liked? It had never mattered before. I was slipping and I wanted something to make me feel validated.

I also chose to use ecstasy because I wanted to escape from the way I was feeling, or to be more specific, to escape from how I wasn't feeling. I was so numb. I couldn't feel much of anything and the idea of this magical drug that could make me feel visceral emotions at a heightened level seemed like an answer, but admittedly a bad one. I just couldn't see this at the time. When it hasn't rained in months you will welcome a monsoon without considering the damage. I took the drug to escape from my numbness, instead of addressing the problem and trying to figure out what was causing it to begin with.

Everything that goes up must come down. Newton said that in a far more graceful way, but you understand the gist. I came down hard from ecstasy. Just as the come up from it is euphoric and mind-bending, the fall is absolute misery – Newton's third law of using narcotics. A profound sadness hangs over you all day, but it is unlike any other sadness because it is virtually unmovable. It sits in your chest and hangs below your eyes and it tells you that you are worthless, and you generally believe it. You live in a total shadow of the night before. It's much, much worse than a hangover, and it's unrelenting. There's no sickness or headaches but there's unbearable lows. You are completely depleted of dopamine and serotonin, and so joy is almost impossible for one very long day. These are not days you should spend alone inside of your head. If you are to do ecstasy at all, be sure that you have plenty of people around you in the aftermath, or ideally a load of dogs. A roomful of puppies is likely to sway you towards some semblance of normality in fairness. Leaving off the drugs entirely is also an option but I'm not going to tell you how to live your life, especially considering I didn't leave it off either.

We went out again on the Thursday night, the final night of Rag Week. I had no desire to do the party drug anymore. I had no desire to even be out and drinking to be honest, but it was certainly more welcome than sitting at home on my own, which was the only available alternative. I didn't want to be alone with my thoughts. My first experience with ecstasy had shaken me to my very core, and unearthed a truth that I had forced myself not to think about for years. But it was too much in plain sight for me to ignore any longer.

As we queued once more to enter a club on Hanover Street among the packed crowds (this time they didn't bother me as I wasn't on drugs), I suddenly broke down in tears in front of my friends. It was as much a surprise to me as it was to them. The sadness grew in me and I could feel it in my throat and before long I was sobbing into my sleeve. It was a release of pent up emotions, all the ones I hadn't been able to feel for so long. In part, this breakdown can be attributed to 4 days on the session with little or no effort to take care of myself. Certainly this played a role in crafting this fragility. Things become far more unbalanced and emotional when you've barely slept, barely eaten and barely drank anything other than beer for several days on the trot. But these tears also struck at the root of why I'd ever found myself in a place where I thought taking those drugs was a good idea. They were tears that had been held back for a long time, ones that Rag Week had broken me down enough to release. I was finally accepting there was something wrong with my mental health, and this was a painful process.

I turned to my friends. I told them I thought there was something wrong and that I might be depressed. They could see it was real, and they somehow felt they'd known it for a while. None of them overreacted or got uncomfortable. It felt like the most normal thing to say in the world. My tears were met with hugs, and hands on my shoulder, and reassuring smiles. A few of them said that it made sense, and that it might be true. Every one of them were supportive and immediately encouraged me to go to therapy, to get help. There was no judgement in them, which is something I will never forget. We were still in the queue for the club, and already I felt better. I had opened up and admitted a truth which had been hidden for years, and my friends had supported me immediately. I felt lucky and humbled to have friends like that. A huge weight fell from my shoulders in that queue, if only temporarily. It was as if I'd been holding my breath without realising, and now found myself sucking in deep lungful's of relief. I wiped away the tears and tried to mentally park the issue until the following day. I went inside the club but after a while I wasn't feeling like being there, so I left early.

The following morning, on the Friday, I woke up somewhat hangover-less, but nonetheless very tired from the week's shenanigans. I sent an email from bed to the student counselling service at UCC and was put on a waiting list to get the help I'd been needing for some time. The rest of that day was spent recuperating and catching up on the many lectures I'd missed. At dinner that evening I told my parents how I was feeling and that I was signing up for counselling. I cried then too. I'd been nervous to tell them more than anyone else. I didn't want my parents to see me differently, to see me as broken. Even though they've always been the most supportive, telling my parents I needed help was always the most daunting part. It always felt like I had to hide this from them – that struggled and felt lonely. At this point though, I was completely burnt out from it all, and had no other choice but to tell them.

They were concerned for me, rather than judgemental as I had feared -- as the anxious mind always fears. I was nervous of what my father might say the most, but he couldn't have been more on board. He told me it sounded like the right move – practical as always. I'm sure my mother cried too, as fears of worse things to come for me appeared on her mind's horizon. They offered me a shoulder, and words of encouragement, and all the things you want to hear when you get difficult things off of your chest. The reluctance to seek help has always stemmed from this fear of being judged, but the people in your corner want you to be open and honest, rather than pretending to be okay when you're not. This is not easy to see when you're going through it, but it is nearly always true.

Saying it out loud, being honest and up front put me back on the right track. Once you can say something out loud it is no longer this vague, gigantic thing in your head. It becomes more manageable when you articulate the way you feel in words because it's suddenly quantifiable. This is why journaling how we feel helps. It allows us to put a limit on the things we feel instead of this heavy weight we have to carry around. What once was an unknown and scary feeling now had a structure in the real world.

I try to explain this concept to people using an analogy of rain clouds. When we keep these things to ourselves, they are like clouds hanging over us, always threatening to rain but never quite breaking. The longer we hold these things in, the larger and darker the clouds become. However, once we put words to how we're feeling, and share them with another person, this causes the rain to fall. The rain can be uncomfortable and painful, but at least once it starts raining you know that it will eventually stop. This is the nature of rain. If you never say the words to someone though, if you keep your pain to yourself, it will never begin to rain, which means you'll never be certain that the clouds will ever go away. They will hang over you constantly until you release your feelings, and release the rain. To make the clouds disappear, and let the sun come back out, you have to allow the rain to fall.

I was 20 years old when I started going to counselling for real. I'd briefly gone to a grief counsellor when Erbie died but this was more a gesture of good will by the school than any actual help. I was also months away from heading on a J1 Visa to Boston for the summer of 2015. My college grades were fine. I had enough friends. I was on a scholarship, I was a semi-decent basketball player. There weren't any parts of my life that were lacking if you were to list off the things someone at that age might desire. You'd say my life was well-rounded. And yet, I was still sad and lonely. From the outside looking in I was excelling, but inside I was crumbling. When I was around other people I was chirpy and up for anything. It was only when I found myself alone that things really fell apart. Dark and horrible thoughts filled my head. I'd be bombarded by insults and words that dragged me down. I hated being on my own because the loneliness and self-contempt would set in as soon as I was.

This is the difficult-to-describe part about mental health issues such as depression. You can have everything going on and still feel low for long periods. The conditions of your life, no matter how good they are, will not prevent you from sinking into depression if you have poor mental health. It doesn't matter who you are, where you're from or how 'good' you have it. If you don't take care of your mental health, it will begin to deteriorate. Celebrities like Jim Carey are outspoken on this, saying that money and fame do not change your depression or your chances of becoming depressed. Material things can't heal a wound you won't allow to heal.

There was something inside of me missing, and everyone else seemed to have it, to own that *it* naturally. I felt hollow. There was little that brought me true joy and happiness anymore. It felt as though I was going through the motions without gaining any pleasure from anything. This seems to a be a story all too familiar, and is often one that can end in tragedy. People said the same sort of thing about Erbie – *"He seemed really happy"* – but you can never truly know. Although I was adamant I wouldn't become one of those tragedies, it's clear to me now looking back, that I was in a bad place and had been afraid to admit it to myself.

When Erbie died I made myself a promise that I'd never go out the same way. I'd experienced first-hand the fall out of such a tragedy. I promised myself that no matter how difficult things got for me, I'd never take my own life. It's a hard promise to make but I had to believe that any variation of pain and torment I could experience was still better than being dead. I'd rather suffer in life than find respite in death. There's a commitment to life we all make that isn't really addressed. We never really celebrate people who commit to living for so long. Life is rarely easy for anyone, but it has to be worthwhile. This commitment to living, despite the pain and the hardship, isn't anything to be scoffed at. We take this undertaking for granted because it feels like the norm, but choosing to live despite all the suffering is a brave decision to make. A commitment to life despite your suffering is bravery, plain and simple. I'm sure this promise to stay alive is the reason I never got to a place where I wanted to take my own life.

I did have some suicidal ideation, where I'd imagine what it would be like to do it, or imagine what it would feel like to be dead. I'd have these vivid intrusive thoughts about throwing myself in front of a car, or taking too many pills. The ideation was more often passive though, and I'd imagine myself getting ill or dying in some freak accident. I'd play out my last days over and over when things were really bad. They were scary thoughts, and felt more curious than they were a plan for action. This ideation would induce intense death anxiety in me too, which we'll get into later. Still, despite all of these thoughts, it never got to a point where I genuinely considered taking my own life. I promised myself I'd persevere and I intended on keeping that promise.

I know how it affects the people left behind. For me, there is nothing too difficult that can happen in my life which is worth causing others' harm in order to end my suffering. I have to believe this is true, and I understand this isn't everyone's brand of suicide prevention. It's not the most politically correct or sensitive, but it's what works for me, and it's the one that I know in my bones to be the most true. Ending my pain immediately isn't more of a priority than the people around me. A collectivist approach to suicide suggests that no matter what happens, your death will do more harm than good for the people around you. Breeding a culture of collective thought rather than individualism may be a way to prevent suicide, as people will naturally learn to consider more than themselves, and potentially understand the impact of their death in a wider perspective.

Suicide prevention is the only aspect of life where I subscribe to a totally selfish and arrogant attitude – It serves to believe I am so valued that my absence would be detrimental to everyone. It becomes a tool to prevent unnecessary death if people can understand how much suffering their permanent absence could cause. Being overly confident of our impact on other people can bring this realisation about. It may not even necessarily be true, but it's a useful tool. Therefore, no matter how bad it gets for me, I will not end my own life because me being gone is worse than anything I could go through personally. I'm not suggesting that a person should just put up with this suffering either – I'm saying there is a way to climb out of the pit of despair without ending our lives, and if we could only understand our impact on other people then we could understand just how loved we are, and just how important it is that we stick around.

I know my suicide would only create a never ending loop of hurt and despair. The only way to break the chain is to make it stop with you, and in order to do so you may need to get yourself some help, because a sick mind can't heal itself.

Up until then, before my experiences during Rag Week, I'd been denying that I had any problems with my mental health. I was actively ignoring negative emotions and covering over them by staying busy. However, it's clear now that I was emotionally blunted and anxiety driven. Things couldn't bring me happiness because I wasn't feeling much of anything. I couldn't extract any joy from life. I threw myself into work and academia to avoid facing my thoughts. I pushed them down and away and told myself I was fine – I was far from fine.

How many people do this? How many of us distract ourselves with jobs, and training, and social media to avoid addressing feelings and thoughts which make us uncomfortable? I'd wager that a lot us do exactly this.

An Inability to Open Up

I hadn't had anything near to a relationship since Erbie's death. I kept myself distant and casual. I justified it in my mind as a phase that most college student go through. I told myself I didn't want to be in a relationship because you're not meant to be in one during those years. This reasoning let me off the hook from facing the real reason. It was a believable excuse but it wasn't genuine. In reality, I was running away from the idea of opening up to someone. It wasn't an option. I couldn't admit to anyone that I was struggling to feel things, because I didn't believe that anyone would want to stick around for a guy who may not be very good at reciprocating emotion. It's difficult to explain this effectively without sounding like you're making an excuse for not trying hard enough. People have often equated not being able to feel these things to not *wanting* to feel them, for not caring. It's an understandable perspective to have, and a difficult one to disprove.

I did want to feel strong emotions but I couldn't, so I took this to mean that I didn't want, nor care, to be in a real committed relationship. Outwardly, I was simply in care-free casual-sex phase. I imagine people thought of me as careless, or a womaniser or a player – but really, I was just too afraid to look at myself directly. Overtime, my relationships became casual and non-serious and superficial. I never really opened up to another person, and I tended to run from situations where feelings began to arise because I convinced myself I couldn't reciprocate these feelings.

I also denied that I was ever doing this. Instead, I told myself I was ending each relationship for genuine reasons and I really believed this. Sometimes this may have been true, but for the most part during my early 20s, I ended things because I was afraid to be vulnerable. I jumped ship as soon as I felt I was getting too deep. I know for certain I hurt a lot of good people. There are many women who felt used or angry or confused as to why I was suddenly moving on from them. I've been on that side of the situation too, so I understand how hurtful it can be. I'd go from being infatuated to ice cold within a few days. So yeah, I hurt some people.

This is an aspect of my mental struggle I didn't come to terms with fully until I was 25, a good four years after I finished my undergrad. I ended so many good things, blaming their endings on trivial shit, when the real reasons were totally on me. Relationships weren't going to be for me because I didn't want to risk the hurt, but this resulted in me passing the hurt onto other people. And I'm not trying to pass up the responsibility of this. I've never been one to excuse bad behaviour because of mental health issues. I was behaving badly and I was struggling mentally, but this does not excuse the behaviour, nor does is it alleviate my role in it. I was still the one who did these things and it doesn't matter whether I was struggling or not because people were still hurt. My point here is, at least now I know why I was behaving in this way, which will help me to improve and grow moving forward.

This reluctance to be in a relationship is tricky because I wasn't ever fully aware of it. It's only through reflection during the last few years that I began to understand why these relationships broke down. In my conscious thoughts back then, I actually wanted a girlfriend. I was constantly jealous of the good relationships all around me. I hated the idea of being alone, but I couldn't ever figure out how to be together. I'd find someone I'd like and then in a few short weeks I'd find myself running from them. Running away from the intimacy of it. Telling myself there was something which rendered the relationship unworkable. I'd find some issue that I made out to be irreconcilable and end the relationship before it became real. I hid the truth from myself, probably so that I'd have some plausible deniability. This happened over and over and over. I'd end a relationship and then months later I'd want that person back again. It was pure toxic. I built people up to versions of themselves which were unrealistic and unachievable. I set unattainable standards and compromised on none of them., rather than accepting people for who they were. I now understand this was a way to prevent myself from being in a vulnerable position. If nobody could meet the standards I'd set, then I wouldn't want to be with them, which kept me from having to lay myself bare. I made sure no relationship would ever succeed.

There is no doubt that many women hate me for it, and I can't blame them at all. I don't like that version of me either. I wasn't willing to accept there was an issue with me and so I never worked on myself. I pointed outwards instead, blaming failed relationships on incompatibility. I told myself the problem was theirs when it was always mine. I framed myself as the victim when I was the one causing all of the damage. The truth is, there was nothing wrong with anyone else, I was just enslaved to my subconscious fear of being in a relationship. This lack of awareness, and reluctance to address my issues, caused a deep loneliness because I felt that I couldn't find a partner and therefore would always be on my own. I was lonely because I wanted to be with someone, but couldn't find anyone. Yet, I couldn't see I was the sole reason nothing was ever working out.

Loneliness can be a weird feeling to manage. It's a fundamental human experience. It comes, I think, as a result of being self-aware, but not knowing how to manage expectations. It can be difficult to pinpoint what exactly is causing you to feel this way. Just because you're alone doesn't mean you'll always be lonely. You also don't have to be alone at all to feel loneliness. You've all heard the cliché turn of phrase *'to be lonely in a room full of people.'* It's overused but it's overused for good reason. Loneliness doesn't come about due to a lack of people – sure I've always had plenty of people in my corner. Loneliness, I think, results from a lack of understanding – a lack of being understood. It wasn't so much that I had no one to date or talk to, it's that I didn't believe I had anyone who could really understand how I was feeling. I didn't think people would be able to understand the numbness, or the inability to feel emotion, and I think this is what made me feel so lonely in the end.

People stop feeling lonely once they know that someone out there gets them, or is at least trying to. And so, when you can't even understand yourself – who you are and what you want – you'll find yourself becoming lonely in your own company too. Not only did I feel nobody would understand the numbness still latching onto me, but I also didn't really understand why my relationships were failing, at least not for the real reasons. If I had understood the genuine cause it would have left me in a position to grow and develop. However, I didn't know, and this left me confused and disappointed, and the lack of understanding left me lonely. And if you get down to the root of both these issues, it's clear that the reason they were happening is because I really didn't know who I was. If you don't know who you are, it's impossible to see when you are behaving in ways that aren't compatible with your essence, and I think this is what happened to me for a long time.

There have been months of loneliness for me throughout the years, which stems from a feeling of being lost, and being without someone who truly knew me. Some days it has felt like there could never be anyone for me, but that will only be true as long as I allow it to be. It's like punching yourself in the face and then wondering why your nose is broken. The evidence was there I just didn't want to see it.

These days there are still periods of loneliness. The only difference between now and then is today I can usually see it coming, and I also know myself better which helps me to fortify against it. Experience is invaluable because once you've been there, you're aware of it coming down the line every time after. I know when I'm beginning to spiral and I can mitigate the damage before it hits. I also know which behaviours make me feel this way, and actively avoid those actions -- casual sex, drinking too much, giving time to the wrong people etc. If you look after yourself properly, and perform real self-care, like doing things that you are meant to do and being disciplined enough to avoid destructive behaviour, you really begin to understand what works and doesn't work. You can use your disciplined self-care routines to stave off any growing feelings of loneliness. Self-care isn't so much giving yourself a day off as much as it's waking up on time, and eating right, and drinking enough water. Self-care requires discipline. It's much easier to survive a storm when you know it's coming, and when you've been preparing for the storm day after day. In my early 20s I felt lonely and sad and anxious all the time but I didn't have any idea of how to deal with it. I didn't fully grasp how temporary these feelings could be so long as I accepted them rather than pretend they weren't happening. In my later 20s I began to understand myself better and so when the loneliness comes for me now, I know how to battle it.

It's hard to admit that you feel lonely when you have so many people around you who love you. You feel like you're betraying them. You feel like it's some sort of disrespectful thing, being lonely in their company. I remember thinking these things. Admitting I was lonely would have been insinuating that the people around me weren't giving me something I needed. But loneliness is not about what other people lack, it's about what you lack. You can feel lonely when you're surrounded by people you love and who love you. When it happens it can feel catastrophic, because it means you're no longer safe from the negative emotions, even in places where you've always felt safe before. Feeling like nobody will understand what you are going through is a very common symptom of mental health problems. You hear this commonly from people going through a struggle – we often think nobody has gone through this, or that nobody will understand how we feel. Yet people have gone through it and they will understand, assuming we give them a chance to do so.

At this time – when I was 21 and 22 – I knew I couldn't feel anything but I didn't think it was an issue. If anything, I saw it as a good thing, and it is only in recent years when I understood to be a problem stopping me from leading a well-rounded life. However, being unaffected by how I felt allowed me one good thing – unwavering focus. The main thing that kept me floating was working towards some tangible and worthwhile project. I had always been good at hard work – instilled in me by hard working parents and brothers – and working towards a goal I felt to be worthwhile kept my mind away from feelings of sadness and loneliness. What's ironic is, finding happiness never seemed to be a goal worth striving for. I didn't even think happiness was something you had to work for, or could work for. I had this idea that it was just something that happened to people who deserved it along the way. There was no effort involved, they were simply happy by default. I figured that if happiness didn't arrive to me naturally then it wasn't meant for me at all. It would take me years to learn that this line of thought was ridiculous.

When I eventually faced up and saw that I wasn't really feeling anything, I knew I was in trouble. There was no sadness, anger, joy, excitement, There was nothing. I was totally numb, and it had been going on like that for years. It took me grinding myself down to nothing, hitting the fever-pitch of a five day bender during Rag Week to realize that things needed to change.

The Lesson

My realisation there on Hanover Street the night I took ecstasy will always stay with me because it was the first time I accepted a version of myself that wasn't beaming, a version that was faulty and in need of help. Up until then I was stigmatising myself for having problems, and hoping they'd disappear on their own. I wasn't gliding through life the way people must have thought. I was running on fumes. I was constantly depending on finding the next goal to achieve. But at least I did realise it. Sadly, some people never become aware that they're self-sabotaging. They never learn that their own worst enemy is themselves. Trying to find happiness whilst telling yourself it is not for you, or that you do not deserve it, and accepting that you will therefore never be happy, isn't what one would call healthy.

Looking externally for something to blame is common, but it is the wrong path. It's exactly what I was doing instead of looking inward to address the route of the issue. The easy road is to look externally and pity ourselves. But you'll never be able to maintain a consistent level of wellbeing if you can't accept your own flaws and the part you play in your own downfall. We all have demons, and monsters lurking in the dark.

The problem isn't that they exist, it's that we don't accept they exist.

You'll never be content if you don't learn to appreciate what you already have, whilst also accepting there are parts of you that may need work. These flaws need to be addressed, but so often we look elsewhere for cheap feel-goods so that we no longer have to look at our own issues. Looking outwards to find value for yourself is futile, because what you find out there will never be enough to prove you to yourself. You have to find your value inside your own mind, and when you find that what's inside of your mind needs work, then you better roll up the sleeves.

I always prided myself on being able to work hard and now, after Rag Week 2015, it looked like it was me who needed the most work. There were thought-patterns to be confronted and behaviours to adjust. There were a lot of hard looks in mirrors to be had. Luckily for me, working hard and grinding it out had been instilled in me by a solid upbringing and years of playing sport. Once I framed my mental wellbeing as a worthwhile goal to be sought after, it became easier for me to work on it consistently. So in the Spring of 2015 I began therapy for the first time. I began to climb back from emotional numbness, and strived towards opening up.

Real Adulthood & Understanding Who You Are

I won't bore you with the details of my personal experience with therapy. Although I'm an open book (quite literally now) there is no benefit to anyone for me to divulge what went on in those rooms. Therapy works because it is private and intimate. In summary, it went well and I learned a lot about myself.

I remember vividly the feeling of relief I got from even signing up to counselling. Taking that first step was huge because it confirmed I was giving myself the help I craved for so long. It was a compassionate thing to do and I felt better for it. I finally showed myself that I actually gave a fuck about my own wellbeing. I attended student counselling in UCC during the first half of 2015, and it seemed to work quite well. I found out things which had been hidden subconsciously so as to protect myself from them. This pesky sub-layer of our conscious minds does a lot of good for us in fairness, but it doesn't get to do those things for free. There's a cost to everything. Although it was protecting me from these darker parts of my mind, it did so at the cost of me being able to form genuine, altruistic relationships. I wasn't actively struggling but I was only half engaged with life, which is no way to live at all.

I learned to spot irrational thought patterns. I learned what emotional unavailability was. I learned how things from my past - the pain of being cheated on, the trauma of losing someone to suicide – impacted the present. Telling my parents I felt unwell and allowing myself to feel the emotions I was pushing down helped me to accept that there were things going wrong instead of pretending like these issues didn't exist. It also taught me that having a mental health problem doesn't change who you are, nor does it mean there is something bad about you. You don't lose your intrinsic value due to suffering. These things can happen to anyone. I framed having a mental health problem as a failure for my whole life up until then, and it only compounded the issue. Not only was I denying there was a problem, I was telling myself that if I did have a problem then there was something wrong with me.

When I started going to therapy, Erbie had been gone for three years, but the effects of his death still clung to me like soaking wet clothes. I had simply been telling myself that the clothes were dry the whole time, whilst falling sick from the dampness of them. Instead of dealing with his death and moving on, like I thought I had, I shoved those feeling down and ignored any thoughts to do with it.

Accepting I was in need of repair allowed me the mental space to actually address what needed fixing, and coming into the summer of 2015 I felt like I'd been given new life. With the help of my counsellor, I'd figured out a way to deal with the lows, to ride out the storms when they came. This is an important distinction – it is unlikely that we will be able to eradicate the presence of lows entirely, but we can arm ourselves to be able to combat them. I felt unstoppable in ways, but as I later found out this feeling of being invincible made me think I didn't need to continuously work on myself. By the time summer came around I felt more secure in who I was , and so I made way for four months in the swampy heat of Boston, MA.

The summer of 2015 is one I'll never forget, but it isn't one that's relevant to the mental health journey we're discussing here. It was a four month period filled with adventure, and new experiences, and hard work, and care-free living. It was good for me in a lot of ways. Working as a mover showed me the extent of my ability to work hard, and I became more resilient as I navigated the world on my own for the first time as an adult. After that summer, Boston became my favourite American city without a shadow of a doubt, and it still very much is.

Once September swung back around, I came home to finish out my final year of college in UCC. I'd graduate with a BA in Applied Psychology in October of 2016, and I'd also leave college with a more firm grip on the depressive bouts I was prone to. I found some sort of balance that I hadn't had since Erbie died, and it brought a huge sense of relief. I was no longer struggling under the grips of a major mental health problem, and I no longer felt the need to hide such things when they did pop up.

However, depression was hardly my most fatal flaw. Depression wasn't the thing which was causing my unhappiness. It wasn't the root of the problem. Depression was manifesting because I was unhappy. And I was unhappy for a melody of reasons I was unaware of. I had figured out a way to manage depression but I hadn't figured out a way to be happy yet. I didn't know who I was or what I wanted to become, which is a very common problem for many young people. I looked everywhere around me to find my purpose but all I saw was false promises.

Very few from my generation seem to have evaded the false pretence of 'being special'. I don't know why or how this came to be. We all have qualities that might make us feel this way – good looks, intelligence, talent etc. – usually none of that is earned but rather, gifted. I have been no different in this sense. Many such things have fallen into my lap, be it by genetic good fortune or simply the universe acting at random. My point being that many of my advantages were never earned so to speak, yet I redefined them as something I had earned somehow, and this is never a good place to begin from.

When the luck ran out, I began to feel lost. College was over, real adulthood was looming, and I didn't have a clue what the next step for me was. I understood then that I would be like everyone else so long as I expected things to happen for me without putting in any effort whatsoever. This is as true for career moves as it is for relationships, mental health, and happiness. Online culture drip feeds us toxic bullshit about the 'Law of Attraction' and how wanting something badly is somehow enough for us to deserve it. This only breeds entitlement, and sets up every single person who does the bare minimum under this idealogue for failure and disappointment. What's worse is that this belief will have people playing the victim, not taking any responsibility when the hammer drops. When failure comes, we often point the finger outwards rather than inwards. In my case, I wanted to be happy and fulfilled and all the rest, but I didn't do any work to figure out exactly what I needed to do to bring this state about. I was manifesting the idea without doing any work. People do this all the time now, but wanting something without putting in the work is a fine way to ensure you'll never get it, and that you'll be miserable when you don't.

At this stage in my early 20s I hadn't even considered writing, and so the blog – *Thoughts Too Big* – didn't exist as my personal script-therapy just yet. Writing has always been important, but I wasn't practicing it daily by then, aside from the work needed for collegiate purposes. I started writing non-fiction at 21 and moved on to include short fiction at 23. Throughout my school years I was always enticed by essay questions in English, and was writing poems and short stories at aged 10 to entertain my parents. The 'writing gene' was there but at this time in my life it was entirely dormant. Even when I started writing, I didn't fully understand what it would become for me, nor how it would help me to find out exactly who I was.

Because I wasn't writing and because I was doing very little reflection, I didn't know what was going to bring me the happiness I craved. I was content enough to exist without diving deep to try and understand who I was. I was happy to choose numbness over sadness and felt that striving for a form of contentment was asking for too much. There was a huge part of me that felt expecting to be happy was like asking for a raise from a boss who wasn't known for giving them. I didn't think I was owed happiness. I didn't know who I was, or what I was about, and this was the issue that was driving me into the ground. How can 'You' be happy if you don't know who 'You' are?

I've always been somewhat intelligent. Intelligent isn't the word, actually. I've always been good in school. Academically I'd have stuff sussed. I'm not very handy with things like my brother or my father, who can throw their hat at anything needing a fix. I'm not the most talented athlete of all time, nor a good singer. I can, however, spin yarns and I know how to take an exam. This isn't the point of the book where I brag about how great I am, but it's important to understand that I'd done well enough in my Leaving Cert exams that I could have done any college course on offer in any university in the country. The irony of this is, I have never been very good at deciding when there is a massive amount of choice. I scroll for hours through Netflix before deciding it's not worth the effort. I'd much rather a choice of two chocolate bars than the exuberant selection at most convenience stores. I can't decide on anything. This has affected every aspect of my life, from choosing a college course to choosing a partner. So, when all courses are an option, this is less of a dream come true than it is a nightmare (I know, poor fuckin' me).

Whereas other kids knew exactly what course they'd want to do when they were 15 years old acting the gowl down the back of class, I was at the business end of a college course and still wasn't sure what I wanted to do with my life. I've never been sure. Nothing has ever seemed to click as making total sense. It felt like nothing suited me totally and I didn't want to simply settle. I picked psychology solely out of interest and wasn't thinking about career paths. But even early on in that, I knew that being a research psychologist wasn't for me. There was a level of guilt that came with this too because in ways I felt I was wasting my parents' money doing a course I was unsure about. For all I know, I was taking up a spot in a course which someone else would have killed for. Someone else would have loved to be there, and I was pitying myself for not knowing what I wanted to do.

I've always been jealous of my older brother in this regard because life just seems to slot into place for him. He's often been gifted with knowledge of exactly what it is was he wants to do. He's always known. There is a drive within him that's simultaneously admirable and jealousy-inducing. Not only does he know what to take aim at, he runs full throttle at whatever the target is. A relentless force of will is what he's always been. Of course, this is just my perspective and is undoubtedly biased and not the full picture. He definitely has his own shite to deal with, too, but my mind always told me he had his shit in order and that's where I drew my comparison. It has always felt like he's been sure of where he's going, which worked to solidify the fact that, for a long time, I did not.

This knowledge, this certainty of what I want, has always evaded my grasp. It still does. The difference now is that I accept the uncertainty as part of me, whereas before I have resisted with great discomfort. Up until recently, I thought that knowing what it is you want in life is the key to happiness. Now I understand that it is not this knowledge that is the key, but rather knowledge of *who you are.* When you know who you are, then you don't worry about the destination, because you understand that you are exactly where you're meant to be. It is only when you are unsure of who you are that you concern yourself with identity, and of where it is you might end up.

There are many things we all have the ability to do, but it is rare that we find things that call to us. And it's even rarer again when we can make a living doing that which calls to us. Things which we are good at, that we enjoy, and that will pay us a liveable wage seem as rare as anything. They are found at the ends of rainbows. As frustrating as it can be to be unsure of what I would like to do, there is no desire within me to settle. There are many examples in my life, and no doubt in yours, of people settling for less than they might deserve, and certainly less than they would like. In my mid-20s, I settled into a job I didn't love for more than 2 years, and it aged me.

It made me bitter and jaded because there was no fulfilment in it. Each workday was full of resentment, as I counted down the hours until I could write in the evening time. I began to get up early to write, too, and I used my day job as a means to keep me afloat until such a time where I was good enough at writing to make real money from it. The lives of other people affected me during this time, because they were *living* whereas I felt I was merely existing. During my college years, I knew full well I didn't want to go down the path of settling, but these things can't always be avoided. I settled for a while, and it sort of dulled my light. I began to fade.

This issue of not knowing what I wanted stretched outside the parameters of education and career as well. I didn't know what type of person I wanted to be. I didn't know who I wanted to be in a relationship with. I didn't know who I was in any sense. I was a man who played basketball and who'd lost a friend to suicide. That was my entire identity at the time. It's what people saw, but I knew it wasn't who I was. I knew there was something more in me, something more than the down and out kid who people should feel sorry for. I hated the idea of being that person, I didn't want people to see me as some sort of victim.

When I can't decide on an option, I usually end up not deciding. I pick none of the above rather than making the difficult choice. I can't make my mind up, so I leave it all go. I can see the correct option for other people quite often, but I can never see which path is the right one for me. And if I am to be more critical, it's not an inability to see the correct path, it is a reluctance to act – because even when you know the right path, it may not be an easy decision to make. It has been my experience that when I know a decision has to be made, I pretend like I don't know what to do, rather than facing up to the harsh reality and acting accordingly.

This has been a problem with my love life in particular, for years. As I mentioned, in college it didn't seem like an issue because I felt it was the time in life when being tied down isn't desirable. There's too much fun to be had and not a lot of time to have it. As well as this, very few people who were in relationships during college are in the same relationships now, which further confirmed to me that I'd made the right call to remain single, or in casual relationships during third level education. However, as I came out of college, I continued to avoid relationships and decisions around them. I could no longer use the *'I don't want a relationship during college'* excuse for dropping the ball repeatedly long into my 20s.

As the years tumbled on, I began to panic because the issue wasn't going away. The reluctance to avoid intimacy wasn't simply a side effect of being in college – the problem lay with me. I could never decide on what I wanted, whether I wanted to be single or in a relationship. It was destructive, both for me and for others. I decided somehow that ending the relationship was the best way to mitigate this potential hurt, because I couldn't keep my eyes from wandering. I self-sabotaged and convinced myself I was doing the right thing for all involved. Instead of choosing to discipline my mind, I chose the easy way out which meant that nothing ever changed. I kept hopping from romance to romance, not giving much thought to what I was doing or who I was affecting. My behaviour never changed yet I got frustrated because the outcomes remained the same. But they would always remain the same so long as I did.

When you don't know what you want in life, what you want out of a relationship, or what you want from yourself, your sense of meaning crumbles. You don't much see the point of droning on day after day with no goal at the end of it all. It's not a reluctance to live, rather it is a lack of passion for anything. You don't want to die; you just lose any sense of fulfilment. Sure, there were always milestones along the way, especially in early life. Finish school, go to college, graduate. As I came towards the end of my first college degree, I realised I'd no clue at all of what I intended to do afterwards. My friends all seemed to have it figured out – some had postgraduate programs sussed, some had ambitions for PhDs, some wanted to work immediately while others set off to travel. This further emphasised the realisation that I was on my own and I began to panic. No one could decide for me, and I couldn't make a decision for myself either. There was a lack of certainty which seemed to come so naturally to everyone else, and it began to feel like there might be something inherently faulty.

Part of me wanted to do each one of the paths laid out by my friends, but that wasn't possible. A huge part of me just wanted someone else to decide for me. With so much heavy lifting involved, I wanted the work to be done by somebody else. There was nothing I felt so passionate about that I knew for definite it was what I wanted to do. I was jealous of friends who had this certainty. I began to feel alone out there on the edge of becoming a real adult. There was only one thing I knew for sure had always called to me, and it was something I always came back to in some form or another – putting difficult to express thoughts and feelings into words on paper. So it was during this time that I started writing.

When Erbie died, I started journaling on the advice of a guidance counsellor. I still have the copybook in my parent's house – a blue lined hard-back with a deep blue cover – and my cheeks burn red with cringe whenever I manage to get through a few sentences of what I wrote in them. You'd probably call this growth, but I call it burn-worthy. Anyway, I wrote letters to him. I began them with 'Dear Erbie' and I signed them off with my name. I never was of the belief that he could read them, but it felt comforting to be talking directly to him in some capacity, even without the hope of a response. Unspoken words that could never actually be heard were at least permanently on paper and away from my mind. It was therapeutic. This practice of getting thoughts out of my head is something I have used often during times when I'm not firing on all cylinders.

I was always drawn to the creative essay. I'd often be able to make up ludicrous plots on the spot during exams and score high. It was something I rarely thought of as a challenge. I actually looked forward to this part of every exam. Having the opportunity to spin words into stories was something I coveted, and I couldn't ever imagine why this was supposed to be part of something that would test us. I had a knack for it. I have always enjoyed using language to convey things that are difficult to articulate. There is a skill in using limited words to convey a very particular emotion. There's a certain magic in it. It resonates deeply when it's done well. And there are so many here in Ireland that display this magic – Louise Nealon, Kevin Barry, Rob Doyle – the list goes on for eternity. Single sentences at the right time in your life can change it forever. Language and writing have this ability.

I felt a great relief when I began to write again. I had a sort of reawakening as to how much it nourished my sense of self when I began writing my blog at age 21. I'd forgotten how much it eased me, and how natural it felt to be doing it. Whenever I feel down or upset or in need of a lift, I just write. I always come back to it in some shape or form. This aspect of writing has always been more important to me than the commercial part of it – writing resonates with me at my core. When I found myself lost at the end of college, writing was something I could do that was of value, which I could see myself doing forever, and so it became my weekly endeavour, and in the years following, it became my daily endeavour.

My desire to talk openly about mental health faded during college. It wasn't that I no longer found it important. I had been going through my own problems, and so trying to do more for others wasn't possible. You can't pour from an empty cup. There have been times when I've done everything I can to help others struggling whilst neglecting my own mental health, causing me to become jaded and worse. I still come back to this idea today, because often I still look out for the mental health of others before my own, and that's a sure-fire way to let your own mental fall into disrepair. You can't help others without first helping yourself. In college I wasn't in a place to help others because I wasn't in a good place myself at times.

As I came to the end of my undergraduate degree, though, the urge to focus more on mental health work came back, like a fire which hadn't been fully ousted. It had been reduced to an ember, and I began to fan it slowly back into a flame. I felt that I could effectively champion for this cause through writing. I have never had all the answers, and I never will, nor claim to, but through sharing my perspective on mental health, my own daily struggles and coping tools, I felt I could help people navigate through their hardships, even in some small way for one single person.

Towards the end of final year, in the middle of my final exams no less, I began a blog called *Thoughts Too Big* and we took on from there. It began as a family and friends reading list, but after a few years, it became a well-known part of the mental health scene in Cork, and today it's an award-wining project. I'm immensely proud of this space, as it became a resource for people to turn to when they need reassurance that they are not alone in how they feel.

The years following my undergrad were busy, and I kind of went on autopilot. I fell back into the comfort of basketball and work, and all the things that make up a busy, modern life. My mental health was very good for long periods and feeling like I was helping people aided that immensely. There was a mental health podcast, started and ended, successfully. I gave talks to various schools and colleges about how depression and anxiety affected my own life. I petitioned local government to get mental health education into the school curriculum (which was successful but fell into the shadows when Covid struck). We did some good in quite a dark time. Suicide seemed to be affecting more and more people as the years went on. And I suppose this reflects what I was focused on, because in reality that suicide rate in Ireland had dropped each year since 2011. Around the time I began to petition local government, it seemed as though there was a suicide in Cork every other day. I went to too many funerals in the October of 2016. Although society was working toward normalising the chat around mental health, there still seemed to be some major roadblocks. Funding and education were the two main ones.

The funding given to mental health from the general health budget every year has been minimal, historically, which means that state-provided services aren't able to help the people who need it most. For example, in 2022 Ireland spend only 5.6% of its health budget on mental health services. The WHO recommends spending somewhere between 10 and 12% on mental health services, but Ireland has rarely gone beyond 7%. For a country that claims to care about mental health, our government's spending appears to suggest the opposite.

Mental health services are only really available to those who can afford to pay privately, which means most people have to wait for months on end to get the help they need. Waiting lists for underfunded state services run the length of the country. We're forced to rely on charities such as Pieta House to provide much needed affordable mental health care. There are of course public services, but you could hardly describe them as adequate. It's easy to see how this is a recipe for disaster. You can't, as a country, claim to care about mental health, yet only allow services to exist for the rich, or for those who can struggle on until their names come to the top of a public list. I have no doubt that a lot of lives could have been saved if our public services for mental health served the people better.

Towards the end of my college days my mental health was cruising. It wasn't bad, but I wasn't working on it on a daily basis – I was coasting. I got complacent with it. I hadn't given myself a mental health routine, something to fall back on when times got bad. Like a country during the economic good times, I wasn't preparing for potential bad times down the road, I was just happy to be enjoying the sunshine of now. However, I was burning it at both ends. In my head, the stint of therapy I did in 2015 had 'fixed' me. I believed that, somehow, mental health problems wouldn't bother me again because I did the time. Much like passing a driving test, I felt confident I would never need therapy again – it was a once-off fix. Little did I know that mental health is something that must be maintained and worked on continuously, because mental health issues can affect you at any stage. This complacency, this lack of discipline, would eventually come back to haunt me.

Just like our physical health, if we don't actively work to maintain good mental health we can lose it. Good mental health isn't just something some people have and others don't, it can be attained through hard work and discipline, much like physical fitness is attained through regular exercise and good nutrition. Issues with my mental health I thought had been magically eradicated slowly began to pop back up. I was still unable to keep up a relationship. I was still running away from everything. I was still unable to express myself emotionally, still unable to feel anything very deeply. The numbness of my mental landscape was still glaring, but I had begun to pretend it was fine again. All of these issues had been painted over with serotonin. Serotonin gained from helping people, and having my writing read, and getting positive feedback from social media – Sources of serotonin which weren't sustainable. My locus of value was very much externalised, and as soon as that validation begins to diminish, or become less effective, so too does this sense of value. Rather than looking inward to define myself, I was looking to others to tell me I was good enough. I hadn't accepted any of my flaws, I was simply looking elsewhere to find my value. If other people thought I was good, then it allowed me to believe it, too. My primary perception of myself was through the eyes of other people for a long time after college, which distorted how I viewed myself and what I considered to be important.

And that is certainly a dangerous idea; the idea that our value is to be found outside of ourselves rather than inside. Instead of working on myself and my problems, I was covering them up by doing 'good' in the eyes of others. In that sense, all the good I did was self-serving. Yes, I was helping people, but a part of me was only doing it to feel good about myself, and that's a serious, and very common problem. There are few, if any, selfless good deeds, but there were times when I wanted to be seen doing the right thing more than I felt obliged to act correctly. And this is a sure sign of an unchecked ego.

The Lesson

When I woke up to the reality that my sense of self was sourced externally, I realised that I still didn't really understand who I was. If I truly understood who I was in depth, then the approval and validation of others wouldn't have been so pertinent. I was hoping to find myself reflected back in the people I was helping, but the image was distorted. The people in my life who really know themselves rarely look outwards to find their value. They already hold it within them, and so what other people think, or what other people do, has no effect on how they perceive themselves.

As I emerged from university and began my transition into becoming a 'real adult' my mental health was intact, but cracking. The fault lines were there. I wasn't experiencing any turmoil consciously but there were still plenty of things I needed to work out. There were still issues just below the surface, churning away and affecting my thoughts and actions. I wasn't doing anything aside from exercise to fortify my mind, and so the collapse into disrepair was almost inevitable, looking back now. All I had to do was allow time to pass, and eventually, those same problems from before -- the loneliness and the depressive spells – would raise their ugly heads again.

Real adulthood was looming. I could no longer make excuses for myself. I was no longer too young to know better, and so every mistake made from here on out was as a result of me not taking responsibility for the flaws in my character. Being a real adult means you have to own the bad parts of yourself and try to make something productive out of them.

Feel Good, Be Good

In September of 2017 I began a Masters of Linguistics in University College Dublin (UCD). The number of students in the class was small and I didn't live too far away from main campus. Some days I walked to college and crossed the crunchy, frost covered pitches to get to class. Most days I cycled the short distance on a bike I'd owned since I was 17. I liked the idea of being in Dublin because it gave me a chance to reinvent myself. I didn't have to be the Daragh I was in Cork, where a lot of people knew me. It's rare that you'd make a trip into Cork City and not bump into someone you know. For all its bravado, Cork isn't a very big place. I was the only Irish student in my class, and one of only two native English speakers, so it was a massive change for me. It was also my first time living away from Cork, the town I was born in. Learning to adapt and respect cultural differences became important to me, and I learned a lot in those months about differences in perspective.

It felt like I could focus on finding out who I was from the inside out, rather than from the outside in. I was living with friends, playing ball with a new team, and enjoying my independence. Every now and then I fell into periods of low mood, but I knew well enough at that stage how to deal with it, and knew that the experience was temporary. This notion is something that I've only grasped properly in recent years. The bad days will pass. They always do, but somehow we convince ourselves they won't when we're in the thick of it. What helped me come to a better understanding was noticing how I never think good emotions will be here forever. I know the good feelings will come and go. Bad feelings, low periods, anxiety, are all the exact same. They'll be here for a while, and they'll leave again just like they always have. Understanding this has been a powerful tool in persevering through days and weeks when I don't feel myself.

However, our mental health isn't something which only affects us, and my time in Dublin taught me that, although I might be feeling good, what I did to feel comfortable could negatively affect other people, which means I wasn't *being* good. Our mental health isn't good if we're feeling fine but we're causing others distress. This suggests that our methods for attaining good mental health are flawed in some way. You can't live morally if looking after your wellbeing results in other people feeling bad. You see examples of this all the time with people who talk shite about others to feel better about themselves. They feel better, yes, but it comes about in the wrong way. We shouldn't have to drag others down to make ourselves feel better. Using people to make ourselves feel better isn't the hallmark of reasonable health. It's a sign that there's a problem.

Although I've never been to the extreme of actively and knowingly hurting others to feel better like some sort of sociopath, I have been inconsiderate with people, putting my selfish needs above the needs of the collective. I have been passively and subconsciously uncompassionate and outright apathetic to other people. I hurt people because I failed to consider how they might feel, rather than purposely trying to hurt them, but the outcome of this is much the same.

Now, we can all be toxic at times. It's inaccurate and unwise to believe that you are never toxic. It doesn't take in the full picture of who we are. The growth comes from an ability to admit that you are sometimes a terrible prick, identifying when you have been, and learning from these experiences. If you behave badly and never acknowledge it, you don't ever grow. You just keep moving from situation to situation, being destructive without accepting any responsibility for your own poor behaviour. I did this for a long, long time. I'd lie to myself and others, pretend certain situations didn't happen, and reframe narratives so I was no longer in the wrong. It's easy to do but we know it's dishonest when we distort facts to make ourselves feel better.

Only in recent years did I reflect on the past and accept that I was in the wrong. For many people I have been the villain. That can be a hard realisation to come to, but it's important to remember that just because we were the villain once, doesn't mean we have to always be the bad guy. Unlike Mads Mikkelsen, we don't have to be type-cast. We can change and learn and be better. This is not a means of leaving ourselves off the hook – if we have behaved badly then that will always be true – but it does allow opportunity to show ourselves some compassion and forgive ourselves for our mistakes.

I thought starting out in a new city might change all of this for me. I was naïve for thinking that. Psychological issues don't disappear based on your address or the weather, or the people around you. The issue wasn't going to go away when I moved to Dublin because I had never admitted there was an issue, and therefore, I had never actively worked on said issue in any capacity.

I was treating people poorly but again, from the outside in, it may have never looked that way. There were no times when I treated people badly directly or on purpose. I was outgoing and chatty and well-meaning. I do believe my intentions have always been good, but like I said, when situations stopped suiting me, I backed out without considering the other person. My bad behaviour was more of the reluctant variety. I'd do things like put off dates or cancel last minute. When we were together and I wasn't keen on it, I became distant and visibly not present if being together in those moments wasn't optimal for me. Being on the other side of that is awful. All of these issues with relationships stemmed from a place of fear. They stemmed from a fear of being hurt.

I didn't feel like I could really trust anyone. I couldn't commit, because that meant leaving myself vulnerable, and the one time I ever did that in the past I got absolutely obliterated. Relationships just became a means to an end for me, and that wreaked havoc on other people, as well as my emotional wellbeing. Sex for me was anything but emotional. It was casual and always made me feel bad about myself because I'd often have no real emotional connection with my partner. It became an entirely physical act of hedonism. I carried a deep shame around with me because of this, and because I was ashamed of how many people I had been with in my life. This again, is something which never seemed to bother other people as much, but it was something I was acutely aware of. This can be attributed to a lingering Catholic shame perhaps, but it's rooted far more deeply in an uneasy sense that what I was doing was morally wrong. A part of me knew it to be destructive which caused the shame. This feeling worsened then when I'd temporarily convince myself I wasn't doing anything wrong and continued to engage with the same behaviours. I'd find myself alone in the aftermath, absolutely disgusted, marinating in self-hatred and resentment.

Whereas it may not have been the case for my partners, sex had become this purely physical activity for me. I'd want to be left alone afterwards which indicates to me that I wasn't engaging with the person, I was engaging with their body. It left me feeling bad, and it left them feeling used and hurt when the relationship inevitably ended. This is the type of thing that will emotionally scar, and it's hard to look back on those years now and have to own the behaviour. That version of me isn't someone I'm proud of but I also have to understand how distorted my understanding of relationships was. Because I hadn't moved on from being hurt, I prevented myself from growing into someone who could open himself up again. This is a difficult pill to swallow. I understand now the errors I made, and for a long time there has been self-hatred for this, because I refused to forgive myself. I wrote myself off as irredeemable and that was it. But you're only irredeemable, I suppose, if you refuse to learn from your mistakes. You're only a bad person if you acknowledge your bad behaviour and continue to behave in that way anyway.

Becoming aware of an issue or flaw is a precursor to progress and growth. Becoming aware that you need a haircut is essential for eventually getting it cut, but the awareness isn't a guarantee that you will visit the barbershop. You still need to act. You still need to do something now that you are aware. Awareness doesn't necessarily equal change. I'm aware of my poor behaviour now and am working hard at improving on it. But in 2017, I was clueless, and I was still chasing relationships even though I hadn't done the work to be in one. There was a part of me enthralled by wanting what I couldn't have.

At a certain point, you have to acknowledge the fact that you're a 27-year-old who has never been in a serious adult relationship. There's nothing objectively wrong with that, but there is for me because I wanted a relationship. I could just never make it work. If you are the common denominator in every situation that falls apart, you are most likely the problem. This needs to be accepted because accepting it is the only way to move forward.

In Dublin, the other issue I faced into again was loneliness. I spent a huge amount of time on my own up there without really wanting to. I've always been inclined towards time alone, but it isn't always a lonely experience. It comes with the territory of writing, really. And there's nothing wrong with being alone. In fact, I generally enjoy my own company and find it to be a good use of my time. However, when you actually want a partner but can't seem to make a relationship work, and when you find yourself alone when you'd really prefer to be around other people, this can cause you to feel lonely.

You don't want to be alone, but you are, and this conflict can be disruptive.

It hurt. It made me feel like there was some part of me which made people reluctant to spend time with me. That's what it felt like, but it wasn't the truth. The truth was I was making no effort to establish and maintain relationships because I prioritised everything else above them. This has often been a problem. I'll begin to feel lonely and self-pity myself. I'll neglect to maintain friendships and wonder why I have no one around. There's a drive in me – an anxiety, really, to always be productive – and this anxiety has caused me to rank work (which is primarily done alone) above everything else. Eventually people get fed up of trying with you, and then, when you do want to be around people, there may not be anyone to turn to.

Jean Paul Sartre once said that, *"if you are lonely when you're alone, you are in bad company."* And I was certainly bad company for long stretches.

When I was around other people I was easy going and fun to be around (up for debate, I suppose) and social. When I was on my own, though, my thoughts became loud and harmful. They told me I was worthless and that I was a bad person. There was too much hate and contempt for myself constantly. My mind told me that nobody liked me, and that they never would. It became a fact that I was unlovable, and that even trying to find someone was futile because there was something deeply wrong within me. I convinced myself of this.

This is the power anxiety can have over us. My thoughts were terrible lies and I believed them. I didn't understand back then that not everything we think is true, and that some thoughts are supposed to be ignored. I didn't even know the true extent of the self-contempt a part of me held. I believed everything my mind told me, and so alone time was often full of anxiety, and feeling of complete isolation. It was impossible for me to sit and relax when I was on my own, and so I was always hammering away at some sort of project to distract me from these thoughts

Dublin was just more of the same old story.

It might have been worse actually, because I didn't have the comforts of being in familiar territory. Oh, how naïve I was to think a change of setting might cure it all. Although I felt it was a fresh start, I quickly fell back into patterns that were all too familiar. Despite feeling like I had changed, I was still self-sabotaging when it came to relationships, and hurting people in the process. I couldn't stop myself, and tortured myself in the aftermath. No progress had been made whatsoever, but because I thought I'd changed, I felt utterly disappointed when I found out I was the exact same as I always had been.

I knew how I was behaving but I never saw an issue with it. I was more concerned with protecting me than I was with how I affected others. It wasn't moral, even though I considered myself to be a moral person. I was the embodiment of hypocrisy and cognitive dissonance. We should care more about how we make others feel than how we ourselves look, but back then all I cared about was getting what I wanted, and I didn't stop to consider how I was making anyone else feel.

For example, I was seeing a girl from Dublin who I neglected to text over the Christmas period when I was back home. Things were going well, and the thoughts of being in a space where I needed to be dependable and open terrified me. She'd take me and I'd simply ignore it. Shortly after my return – after several weeks of minimal communication – I matched one of her friends on a dating app and we began chatting casually. I knew she'd find out, and that this was how we'd end things. I was a full-blown asshole but I know I rationalised it as acceptable back then. I told myself I wasn't in a relationship and so didn't need to explain myself to anyone.

Our situation didn't work out as a result of me being scared and unwilling to communicate, but I never gave her an explanation. Instead, I continued to talk to her friend and forced the relationship to implode. On some level I felt like I deserved to be hated by her, so I made sure that I was. Who the fuck does that? There were so many other women to chat to if that's what I really wanted, yet I felt inclined to chat to one of the only girls who was off limits. In my mind it was a punishment for me – and the way I felt after did feel like punishment as I was ravaged by guilt and shame and deep hatred for myself. Still, I was hurting a girl who didn't deserve it far more, and her only crime was genuinely liking me.

I punished her for liking me. That says a lot about the person I was.

Similar behaviour repeated itself over the better part of a decade. It was a warped defence mechanism against getting hurt myself. I self-destructed over and over to stop myself from getting to a place of vulnerability. Although not every relationship ended because of my behaviour, or lack of caring, most of them did. If you could check out the stats, often a good thing ended over nothing, because I wouldn't work on myself.

As a result, a lot of good people got hurt. Many still despise me to this day, and with good reason. I don't like the person I was either.

This is what I mean by *'good'* mental health not being exclusive to how we ourselves feel. I was feeling good, and evading relationships, and hurting other people in the process. It felt like the correct move for me, as it kept me inside of my comfort zone. Even though I *was 'protecting my peace'* and salvaging my mental health, I was wreaking havoc on the mental health of others. This is not a sign of good mental health. This is maladaptive. This is the sign of a narcissist who will use and sacrifice other people in order to feel good about themselves. This is what I was doing during this period of my life. For too long I believed that my peace was the most important thing, and that I should attempt to get it at all costs, which is an awful perspective. But it has also become a very common way to look at things, and it's often dressed up as self-care.

Our happiness and well-being is partly dependent on other people, and theirs is partly dependent on us. So in that sense, our focus should be on the collective well-being rather than on our individual happiness. When we help others it makes us feel better. When we are selfish we often get feelings of imposter syndrome or doubt or guilt, because we put ourselves above others in the wrong ways. Social media normalises this behaviour, but it is not the way to consistent contentment. You can't solely prioritise yourself and your own desires and expect others to care about you. You can't prioritise everything you selfishly want over your relationships – that's what I did and look where it got me. It got me a decade of being alone. This way of thinking is not conducive with well-being. This notion of 'self-care' which normalises narcissism will not make you happy. In fact, it will do the exact opposite.

The Lesson

After Erbie died, I gave myself a Get Out of Jail Free Card. Any behaviour of mine was justified because I was, somehow 'damaged'. I could explain any bad decision away with mental health issues or trauma. I didn't do this consciously, but it was an excuse for me to not take responsibility for my actions. I believed I was broken for a long time and that this brokenness was the reason I was hurting so many other people, and it was also the reason that this behaviour was in some way acceptable.

I refused to take any sort of responsibility for myself. I didn't think I had to. In many ways, I was utterly pathetic and I'm still learning to accept that. There are still ramifications from the fallout. I was using Erbie's death as an excuse to be a terrible person to some people, and this is despicable.

A mental health problem is no excuse for being a bad person, but I know that for a long while, I was able to reconcile the bad behaviour in myself by telling myself I was broken.

Some of the people I dated from 2017 and 2018 in particular will hate me forevermore. I deserve that. It reflects the person I was at the time. I like to think I'm no longer that person, or at least, I'm actively trying not to be. Even now, on nights when I can't sleep, these memories play over and over in my mind, tormenting me, trying to convince me that I'm a bad person. It can be challenging, and indeed painful, to accept our misdeeds, but to also know they are not a true reflection of ourselves. If we can learn from our mistakes then at least we're trying to improve.

I've always said that a bad person never considers whether they're bad or not. I also don't believe that anyone is fully bad or fully good – we're all a mix of light and dark. I've noticed that people who are mostly good tend to think they're awful people quite often.

There's a level of guilt and shame for even the slightest misbehaviours. In good people there's a drive to, at the very least, try and do the right thing. I think it's important to remember this when we make mistakes.

If we misbehave and feel remorse or guilt for it, it's a sign that we have a moral compass, and that we know what we did was wrong. If we don't feel any sort of internal conflict when we treat other people badly, then we may have a more serious problem. I'm flawed for sure. I have my shortcomings, and these shortcomings and flaws are my responsibility – not anyone else's. Today, I can say that I'm trying, I really am. I'm no longer leaving these flaws in the dark, hoping they'll disappear. So although I've treated people poorly in the past, I'm trying to make up for it now by attempting to better myself. I must believe that counts for something. We all fuck up at times. That's life. What's important is that, when we do, we own the bad behaviour, try to understand it, learn something from it, and grow.

Side Note on Writing

During the year of my Master's degree in Dublin I started doing some more serious writing.

And by serious writing I, of course, mean that I started writing fever-dream short fiction about the type of thing that could never happen as a means of procrastinating doing my thesis. Fairies appeared before Instagram fitness types, priests had bright blue balls, and grown men turned into inanimate pieces of celery. I'd never considered fiction before, but it had found me in the darkness, and this kind of writing became my personal therapy.

I found seamless hours of flow in the creative process of it all, and I knew that I'd honed in on something which spoke to me on a deeper plane. There was a stage during the last gallop of that degree where I had more words written for my first book's manuscript than I had for my thesis. This confirmed that I had found my path. Priorities were clear, if not misdirected. Writing was my escape from daily life, and it allowed me to find a sense of fulfilment during a time when I was still unsure of who I wanted to be.

I'd been blogging and doing some freelance work for some years by then. I wrote for UCD's Observer throughout my postgraduate degree, but none of that held a candle to the way creative writing made me feel. The spark I used to feel in English class during my teenage years reignited, and I understood then that this was something worthwhile, and something I had to pursue. It clicked with me like nothing else ever has. Suddenly, I understood how my peers felt after college when they knew exactly which path they needed to be on. Writing creatively gives me a sense of flow and meaning like nothing else. When I was younger, basketball provided this for me, but now writing had overtaken this in a definitive way.

Writing is therapeutic. It allows one to use pain and torment to paint dreadfully meaningful pictures – real things which people can feel vibrating off the page. However, it also allows me to fall back into romanticising my flaws. It allows me to believe I need them for the sake of the art. I began to wonder whether my writing would suffer if I wasn't anxious or in a low mood. I started to question whether I actually needed to feel bad so that I could be good at this newfound passion. This streak caused me to find solace in the low days, and the long weeks of anxiety. At least when I felt bad it meant that the writing would be good. Whatever way you look at it, finding writing did improve my mental health, and it continues to be a tool I use to maintain my wellbeing.

It brings stability to my life. It brings meaning. I know that if all else fails I can still find value in putting words down on paper, if even for an hour. I finally had some long-term goal to strive for. I was no longer going from achievement to achievement, hoping one of them would bring me the impossible satisfaction I so desperately craved. Now, I had my thoughts focused on the written word, and I felt I could help people in a meaningful way with them. It also felt like a well which couldn't run dry, because there will always be something for me to write.

At last I found the thing which others seemed to find so easily – I found a passion for something.

I finished out my masters in the autumn of 2018, but it no longer seemed as important. Still, in linguistics I learned a lot about language and how to change and manipulate it to engage different people. So this education informed my writing in a profound way. What was important from then on was writing and nothing else. It's all I could focus on. Even basketball lost some of its shine, and I had been infatuated with the sport since I was 10 years old. I graduated in the winter and picked up a job to pay the bills doing linguistic testing work. It was uninspiring but it allowed me the freedom to write as much as possible, so I didn't mind.

The year of my masters was the year I found out what I wanted to do. I found the best part of me, in a time when I was also behaving selfishly and destructively, hurting some good people in the process. When we hear about people we admire, we rarely hear the bad parts, and even when we do, we minimise their faults. The flaws make the person, so they say. It's true with ourselves, too.

I found something that worked for me that year. A light to guide me through all the shit. Writing has allowed me the ability to effectively address my problems. I wouldn't know how I was hurting people, or how my behaviour was toxic without the help of writing. It's a gift I hope I never take for granted.

The Lesson

Even when I go through bad mental spots, I always lean on writing to guide me home. It's a constant in my life. Writing won't be for everyone, but I would implore you to find your thing - your constant – whatever *IT* that will drag you through even if you don't feel like it some days. We all need something which can help us to persevere through our darkest days.

Find your passion, and do it because you love it.

When you find it, never leave it go. Nurture it and keep it close. The rest will come if it's meant to. It should never be about the praise, or the accolades, or the success, but only about the doing of it, because it makes your heart alight, and because it brings hope when there may not be a lot of it going around.

Find the thing which brings meaning to your life, and acknowledge when you're being a prick: That's the lesson I learned from the year I spent in Dublin.

Addressing the Shadows

Let's skip ahead a few years.

Between 2018 and 2020 I kept the head down. I worked and I wrote and I played basketball. That was sort of it. My mental health was as steady in those few years as it's ever been. This isn't to say we shouldn't acknowledge the good times, but I'm certain you know how to relish in good feelings. Everyone can talk about a time when they've felt happy. This book is about normalising laying ourselves bare and addressing flaws. Putting all the flaws and problems and struggles out there in the open is something we generally feel reluctant to do, and so I will endeavour to do just this. During this time I hadn't necessarily worked out the kinks of my most persistent flaws but I was trying to live more in the light. I avoided leading people into relationship-ish situations. At the very least, I knew I was bad at relationships so did the utmost to keep away from trouble.

I don't think I need to remind you of what went down in 2020. The pandemic had a profound effect on our collective wellbeing, in every sense of the word. Physically, mentally, socially, financially – whatever aspect you can think of – we were all struck down and held there for well over two years. These next few realisations occurred during this time, so it wouldn't paint the full picture if I neglected to address COVID-19. That being said, this part of the book isn't about the pandemic, it's about *mental health* during the pandemic, which is necessary to talk about.

I moved into an old house on the Douglas Road in Cork towards the end of May in 2020. It was a blue house with weeds in the front garden and no ironing board. The house itself was an ancient structure. Fresh coats of paint had concealed its deep wrinkles and imperfections, which had drawn out their length over time like everlasting candles. The place creaked and moaned and complained. It was lopsided and both too cold and too warm in different rooms. Nothing in it worked perfectly but everything did in fact work. A few months after we moved in, during a particularly epic downpour of saturating rain, the wall between the kitchen and utility room started pissing water as if from some cliché horror movie. Realtors would describe this house as having character, but it's more accurate to describe it as neglected.

I ended up living here for the bones of two years.

It was a strange time to begin with, and moving in there was strange, too, but it felt good. We'd come through the first wave of the pandemic and restrictions were easing off so much so that life felt like it might soon return to normal. At this point you could meet people and sit outside for coffees. The weather had been a blessing, and the morale had a hopeful flare to it. Initial fears of the virus diminished, and we all took our chances with reasonable risk rather than obeying rules to the word.

At the time, I was meant to be lost on purpose in South America somewhere but the virus of 2020 put a halt to that. That was a trip I'd been planning for a year and a half. It's my own fault for making such public plans – the universe got wind of them and decided there was another path for me to take. Almost unbelievably, I had intended to hand in my notice in work at the end of the same week in March we were told we'd be working from home indefinitely. Something in my gut told me my trip would be cancelled so I held off on quitting.

A few short weeks later all international flights were off the cards and any chance of my trip going ahead faded into oblivion. It was annoying, but missing out on a trip of leisure I could personally pay for is the definition of a First World problem, and so although I was disappointed, I knew it could have been far, far worse. I took this development in my stride in fairness, and the news didn't affect me too negatively. When the trip was cancelled, the pandemic was still very new and exciting and scary, so it didn't feel so much like I had lost out. It felt like the sensible outcome.

When I feel trapped, or when I feel like I'm becoming stagnant, I tend to make impulsive decisions without fully thinking them through. When it feels as though I have no say in what's going on, I tend to drum up some situation where I do have some say in the matter. I had no say in what was dictated by the pandemic, but I could take control of things directly within my vicinity.

Taking some sort of control back when the world around us is unpredictable and chaotic makes us feel more at ease. It soothes the mind. We tend to crave control in general, so when things spiral out of our control, or when we never had control to begin with, it can cause us to become anxious. We can become fixated on the things we can't change.

I remember when I was very young I obsessed over the world ending. It scared me to think it could just end out of nowhere and I didn't want this to happen, obviously. However, because I had no control over it, I anxiously thought about it every day. The thoughts consumed me. It controlled me because I couldn't control it. The fact that a terrible thing could happen, and I couldn't do a thing to prevent it caused a deep sense of terror in me. This happens to varying degrees whenever we find ourselves in uncomfortable situations where we have no control.

In order to overcome this anxiety spiral, we can focus on things remaining within our control. These are often things like our mindset, our physical fitness regimes, our habits etc. – anything which can be influenced without requiring external factors. Finding control in amongst the chaos can bring back some semblance of structure, and this helps to prevent us from sliding back into poor mental health. Controlling a small part of an uncontrollable and chaotic world helps us to stay grounded.

Over the years, this need for some control has resulted in impromptu holidays, solo pilgrimages, last-minute nights out, tattoos, radical haircuts, and so on. These types of impulsive decisions have been for the most part harmless, and have allowed me to take back control in times when I feel I have none of it. Moving into that lopsided gaff on the main Douglas Road was one of these decisions. It felt like I was at least deciding some of my next steps rather than being dictated to by a chaotic universe.

I had been living at home with my parents since finishing my masters to save for travelling. Now that my trip was scrapped, I felt like I had lost all sense of purpose, so I decided within a week that it was time to move out. The trip to South America had been my sole goal for the year, and so when it fell through I felt lost because I had no Plan B. That had been the only plan and now there was no alternative in place.

Panic descended.

So I left my parents' house nestled in the warmth of the countryside and I moved into a house on the main road there, not far from the Briar Rose Bar. It was a well needed break from the confinement of lockdown at home. Almost 3 months had passed in virtual social isolation. In the beginning it was novel and the idea of doing quizzes online with friends was comical. The virus was new and scary so being in lockdown felt right. It felt good. We all felt heroic in some way, like we doing the right thing for the greater good.

Don't get me wrong either, I get on very well with my parents. We have great time for each other. But living with parents isn't optimal for any adult. You can't talk to parents about the same things you can talk to your friends about, at least not to the same degree, nor with the same details. Parents also have the uncanny inability to understand why one may not wish to be around them 24/7.

Space is needed, and even more so during a global health crisis.

As time went on there was only so much of lockdown in the family home I could take, with no one else my age within a few miles. My brother lived in Dublin at the time, so there was no chance of bouncing off of him either. I was drinking too much out of sheer boredom, as well as finding it difficult to motivate myself to work.

When every day feels the exact same you start to wonder if it's all worthwhile. Doom starts to seep in slowly in the night as you wonder whether life will end in this disturbed Groundhog day you now find yourself living in. You wonder if life will ever return to normal, if it even ever could. It can get bleak quick, as weeks seep into months and suddenly you're having a birthday in lockdown. Now you've actually aged during an event which was supposed to last three weeks. So when an opportunity came to break the cycle of doom, I didn't hesitate to take it.

I moved in with some friends from school, and that first weekend was a giddy affair of drinking indulgently. Those nights felt entirely normal again, which was a welcome change. We forgot for lengthy moments that the world was upside down. I could hear the cars and buses pass on the main road as I settled into bed, a feature which didn't exist in the countryside. There was a 24 hour bus service that passed right by our house, like an hourly reminder of the city. The big woosh and tumble of urban life. I can't remember a single night where I couldn't find sleep because of the passing night coaches.

I had stopped keeping up with covid numbers almost entirely by then. The start of lockdown, and particularly when I was living at home, all we could do was watch as the daily numbers rose steadily around the globe. It sapped any hope of the pandemic ending. You'd be surprised how much your anxiety will decrease without knowledge of a thing, though. Ignorance may not be bliss, but it can be beneficial. You can lead an almost normal life in an abnormal world if you restrict yourself from access to the news. By then I started to understand that watching news media was basically consenting to feeling bad as frequently as possible. News cycles are non-stop reams of awfulness. Bad news follows bad news in a never-ending sea of despair.

It's designed this way. It's designed to make us feel helpless and stressed.

It's far more difficult to feel hopeful whilst subscribing to such things. Your thoughts begin to align with the tone of whatever you consume, so watching the news makes our thoughts become pessimistic and hopeless. Once I stopped watching the news, my awareness of the horrible things that happened every day minimised. I no longer subscribed to negative things which I had no control over. My thoughts became more localised, and as I focused more on the things within my control the state of the world became far less overwhelming. The lads would often suggest that these were things I ought to know about. The internet told me it was somehow immoral to ignore certain global events, too. But this is just a form of emotional manipulation, a tactic used by those who are already within a belief-system.

The truth is, my knowledge of an event holds no bearing on its occurrence. It makes no sense to make yourself worry about events which you have no control over, events you cannot stop from unfolding. If there is something you can do, then absolutely do it, but having an emotional attachment to events happening thousands of miles away serves no good purpose, and it will disrupt your own wellbeing.

Care? Yes, but allow yourself to feel bad? I don't think so.

Whatever you do, these things will happen. Such is life. Mitigating how much evil you intake on a daily basis isn't immoral, it's self-preserving. So I stopped opting in for the feel-bad cycle the news provided, and this seemed to make the whole situation feel much better. There was a marked reduction in stress and feelings of panic about the future. Covid only existed in my life when it directly entered it, like when masks needed wearing or when people I knew got the virus, or when I became a close contact – and these things didn't happen so often as to suggest Covid was taking over my life, or indeed the world.

I think the most difficult part of lockdown at home was the lack of interaction socially, and specifically, interactions with the opposite sex. You could fill the void of friendship well enough with online interaction and phone calls and video chats and quizzes. The craic can be had in decent proportions without seeing the other person face-to-face in real time because you already had years of time invested in the friendship. It's not equal to in-person contact but you can make-do temporarily maintaining friendships in this way.

However, as you know, there are a lot of elements to a romantic relationship which require in-person contact, and this includes far more than just the sexual aspect of it. It's difficult to gauge someone without standing in front of them. There are many subconscious queues, and pheromones, and all the rest of the biologically driven malarky, which are lost via the internet. Dating in a world where meeting someone in person is outlawed is a challenge, and often it feels more hassle than it's worth.

In the pandemic, you generally already had the friends you had, and they'd a good grasp of who you were, so these friendships were easy enough to facilitate online. However, if you were single like I was during that time, it was incredibly difficult to meet someone because all knowledge of the person came from online interaction, and this can be very skewed if you've never met the person in real life. We've all been there, when a person is one way online and totally different in person. They don't talk as much, or they look different to their pictures. It can be a minefield. So if you only know a person online there's a good chance you don't know the person at all. Sure, you can get to know their likes and dislikes and all the semantic knowledge of a person that will of course be true. But you don't get a sense of their energy, or their demeanour or their 'vibe'. You learn more about a person from how they behave than you ever will from how they type, or what they say they like to do in their spare time, and so meeting in person is fundamental, at least to me anyway.

Beginning a relationship, or even trying to find someone during a pandemic is nothing short of impossible, especially when you live at home with your parents. The amount of talking stages (which is just texting a person for a few weeks to get to know them) that fizzled out into nothing during 2020 made me reluctant to even try, because nothing was going anywhere.

I'd been single for some time by then as you know. Casual relationships were frequently part of my life, whether that's a good thing or not (it's probably not). I used them often as a means to subdue any growing feelings of alone-ness. It wasn't a healthy view of how relationships should be, but that's where my head had been stuck for quite some time. I still panicked at the first sign of commitment.

I had grown to the point where I directly told potential partners that I wasn't looking for anything serious. So although I was being a coward, I was being an honest coward. It was progress, I suppose, but I was still avoiding the baseline issue entirely. Instead of trying to figure out why I was afraid to commit, I was openly admitting that I wouldn't commit. It's better than leading people on, but it's far from ideal. As we've gone over, there was still a part of me that was terrified of being hurt, and so my answer to this was a string of casual relationships rather than finding anything meaningful. It's a pretty bleak and hollow form of love, and it doesn't lead to anywhere but loneliness.

Being out from under the thumb of the parental home means you can at least have a place you're not petrified to bring a date back to. There's no sneaking around involved, which is a grand thing. Believe me, I'd been walked in on enough times with a 'friend' in bed to know it was not something I'd like to repeat. The level of awkward embarrassment at dinner tables during the weeks that followed such encounters was not worth it.

My view of sex had become transactional rather than bound to emotion, which had been a problem for years under the surface of it all. It was an ignorable problem, though. I'd liken it to a sickness you know you have but aren't treating, or a toothache that you hope will just fuck off in time. That's how I felt about my wellbeing issues. I hoped to God that if I just put up with them long enough they'd go away. They'd evaporate like puddles in the sunlight if I just gave it time. However, an emotion unexpressed is one that toxifies and becomes distorted. They don't just disappear. And this relationship flaw I held down so firmly was fully rotten at this stage.

Because I'd cut myself off from the possibility of commitment for so long, it warped my definition of sex. Rather than it being an expression of love, it became a purely physical and carnal engagement, which leaves you feeling numb and empty one way or another. That isn't to say I was looking for someone to use for the sole purpose of sex, though. In the conscious reaches of my mind that is never something I ever decided upon. In fact, I still believed I wanted a relationship. It still wasn't clear to me that I was afraid of commitment, rather I convinced myself I had reasonable reason to run from each relationship. I put the blame on the other person every time rather than facing up to my own issues. Being quite a guilt-ridden and introspective person, I find it quite harsh on my mental health to engage in meaningless sex. The idea of organised sex without any real intimacy makes me feel deflated and empty. It's a big part of the reason the idea of paying for sex is never one I've considered. Sex for the sole purpose of sex feels bad to me, but sometimes it does happen. I have done it, and often enough I come out the other side attached to some sort of moral crisis. I always end up in a spiral of self-hate that disrupts everything else in my life. It makes me feel bad or impure for some reason.

Much like a headache, not much can be enjoyed whilst you're under this shadow of guilt. My intention is never to have sex and then for the relationship to end shortly after, but this has happened regularly.

Generally, I'll meet someone and become entirely infatuated. I'll be obsessed almost. I'll convince myself for a brief time that I've found something akin to 'the one'. This leads me to seeing this person too often in too short a time-span. We'll overdo it, and I'll burn out whatever romantic feeling I had towards them, or I'll find that we're not as perfect for each other as I initially believed. Even though it's my own doing, I'll begin to resent being around them, despite the fact that it was I who'd suggest hanging out. Essentially, I'll grow to dislike some minor facet of them faster than I learn to like their person. There'll be some arbitrary thing I can't let go, and it is this inability to let a small thing go for the sake of the relationship that is the manifestation of my fear of commitment. This is a truly horrible part of my person, but it does exist, so it needs to be addressed.

It has happened too often with me for it to be anyone's fault but mine. It's not a good way to live, especially when the cycle doesn't break. For quite a long time I lived in the fantasy that it would be *'different the next time around'*, but when you make no attempts to fix a problem it is completely ludicrous to think it will just fix itself. The *'next time around'* was never different because I never changed.

Instead the same outcome repeated itself.

The summer, I moved out with my friends was no different, despite the context of the pandemic. Despite all the progress I'd made in dealing with low mood and anxiety, I had never addressed my relationship issues, and so nothing had changed since college, a good 5 years in the past.

In July I met a girl online.

We had some friends in common and hit it off immediately. We got on great if I'm honest. We laughed. We enjoyed each other. Then after a few short weeks things became stale quite rapidly. Neither of us had an urgent desire to see the other. There were things we both wanted to say but didn't. Communication was a problem. I became distant, putting off dates instead of talking to her about it. We decided that we should just be friends, both knowing that it was unlikely we'd ever hang out again. A few weeks later she blocked me on social media and that was that. The more underlying issue throughout this, and throughout previous failed relationships was that I felt unsure, and frankly, afraid of committing. I wasn't sure about her but I didn't give it a chance, nor did I tell her how I was feeling. I have regularly found reasons to not be with a person because, all of a sudden I go from wanting a relationship to wanting to be left alone. It's a fight or flight response to a situation which might make me feel vulnerable. Instead of standing my ground and moving past it, I run every single time. I panic and hide instead of seeing where things might lead to. It causes me to feel deeply upset because it sometimes feels like I'll never be able to manage a relationship with anyone. This feeling was especially intense when I didn't know what the problem was. Now that I do, and am working on myself more consistently, the feeling doesn't control me as much, and I feel like I may be able to engage in a healthier way.

I was living in the house about seven weeks by the time this first budding relationship ended, and I felt utterly outside myself in the days following. It felt as though I was observing a man from a distance, knowing what it was he was doing wrong, yet not reaching out to help him so that he might live better. I just watched how destructive I was being, feeling bad for myself rather than doing anything to stop it. I wasn't doing much of anything other than allowing myself to succumb to primal urges. There was no discipline, and frankly, very little self-respect.

It's been difficult to come to terms with this marked flaw. For most of my adult life I've pushed it away and have kept making excuses for its existence. I kept hoping it would just go away when the right person came along. I kept hoping that someone else would do the work for me. Things don't just magically go away, though, and nobody can heal us but ourselves, no matter how much we'd like them to. It was on me – it's still on me – to take responsibility and stop hurting people because I'm afraid to see my own issues for what they are.

An ex of mine once told me years ago that I only ever want what I can't have, and once I get it, it's no longer something I want.

It reminds me of a Joker quote from The Dark Knight – *I'm like a dog chasing cars, I wouldn't know what to do with one if I caught it.*

I'd just told the same ex-girlfriend, in drunken openness, that I still loved her. Actually no, that was the first time I'd ever even told her I loved her. She had a boyfriend at the time. I loved her because I couldn't have her. I told myself she was wrong and that she didn't know me well enough to make that call. A couple of months later, when she became single again, I suddenly had no interest because she was no longer unattainable. What was I hoping to accomplish by telling her that I loved her? Was I hoping that she'd be elated and run off with me? Probably, which is proof that she was right about me.

Would any of that have made me happy? Not at all. The goalposts would have moved and I would have lost interest as always because the issue was never the availability of the other person, it was always with me getting cold feet once I got what I wanted. In that situation, she would have left him for me, and then a few weeks later I would have left her because I didn't want her, I wanted the idea of her. I wanted her to want me, but I wasn't going to commit because I was too scared. It's always amazed me that she could see so clearly what was hidden to myself. Hidden is perhaps the wrong word considering I knew it was there but refused to look. She addressed a flaw when all I could do was run away from it.

So in a more honest sense, it wasn't that things had fizzled out with this woman during the summer of 2020. It was more so that I didn't wish to commit because my eyes travelled elsewhere, to potential relationships with other women that may have been 'better' for me. My reluctance to commit stemmed from two sources – the first was fear as we have discussed, but the second was a difficulty focusing on one person. I couldn't aim at one relationship and stay the course.

When you think about this for a single moment you'll understand it to be a subtle form of insanity, because it ensures one will never find something worthwhile. One would never be content with any relationship if this were to be the overriding outlook – that there is always someone better suited. Even if this is true, it doesn't serve any benefit unless you're in a relationship that is detrimental to your health or wellbeing. I couldn't commit to one person because the possibility for something more suitable was always there. And it will always be there. There was a huge internal conflict, and it forced me to stay alone because fighting against this urge to look while trying to settle seemed too difficult a thing to do. This had been my passive attitude for so long that I was no longer certain of what it felt like to be utterly enthralled by one person, and one person alone.

My awareness of these relationship issues finally came to a head in 2020. But as is the recurring theme, awareness of something doesn't automatically guarantee an aversion to the behaviour. You can know that you need to stop eating so much to lose weight yet continue to overeat out of habit. You need more than just awareness to alter a behaviour. It's a good start, I'll give you that, but it's not so simple. When it comes to how we feel, it becomes even trickier. I finally understood that the desire to run from a relationship was irrational and harmful, but that didn't alter the way I felt, and I often felt I no longer had feelings for the person in question.

Relationships die when this switch flips – you begin to resent spending time, and you lash out and cause problems where there are none. You become distant and inconsiderate. When it happens it is either me who ends the relationship, or I become so cruelly distant that the person I'm with ends it instead of putting up with my bullshit. The situation becomes too unaccommodating to stick around. There's no way to resuscitate it.

The week following the pseudo break-up (I say 'pseudo' here because we weren't exactly going out, but it was long enough to warrant a definitive choice to end things) a girl I'd had a crush on in the past messaged me out of the blue and asked if I wanted to meet up. It was unexpected and surprising, but of course I said yes because I was almost instantly back in a place of loneliness, even though it had been my decision to be alone. She picked me up one hungover Sunday evening, and we drove and chatted for a few hours. We walked on a nearby beach and talked about superficial things. Nothing happened between us, nor had I really wanted anything to in the moment. We had nothing at all in common. She was too focused on making people jealous on social media – which she demonstrated by driving us to a beach for the sole purpose of taking a picture to post it on her story – and I was too focused on abstract things that would have bored her.

It struck me on a weird note, though. This was a girl I had been dying to hang out with for some time and when it actually happened, it amounted to nothing. Once again, I got what I wanted and then I became uninterested immediately. I guess I didn't really have as much of a grip on who I thought I was as I might have liked. The prophecy my Ex had made all those years ago continued to be bang on.

The weekend following this date was an absolute belter. It was the type of July weekend where you'd be sweating just sitting still out in the garden. Sunburn was back in stock and people were around the place with red necks and stinging backs of the knees. It was the type of heat Irish people find themselves complaining about. I went for a run on the Saturday morning before the dead heat of midday struck, and then went to watch a 5km time trial race with my brother in the afternoon. In the evening we headed down to the parents' house for a BBQ with my parents, my brother's soon-to-be in-laws, and his own girlfriend. It was the sort of day you'd find yourself remembering fondly.

There were talks of relationships then, as there usually is when three couples get together. Jokes were made at my expense as always, and an uncomfortable silence followed naturally. Three happy couples were perplexed at my lack of a relationship status. I remember considering telling them that being single was a relationship status. I remember choosing not to go off on a tangent to explain that being in a relationship doesn't make you 'right' and being single doesn't make you 'wrong'. I didn't bother in the end. I just laughed and sipped from my beer and pondered over the close-mindedness of the way our standards for happiness are structured.

There's a sense, as nuanced and subtle as it is, that our society views single people as having something wrong with them. This feeling becomes more obvious the older a person gets, as people start wondering why they never got married or if there might be some fatal flaw. There is nothing objectively wrong with being single but people will make you feel like there is. They make you feel as though you're somehow failing because you're single. Maybe it's true, and the reason it irks me is because it feels like an honest attack.

A telling look, or an awkward silence will confirm to you when people feel pity because you are without a partner. It's as if people think happiness could never be found in a meaningful way without an other half. There's too much weight put on relationships, and this more often than not makes people feel sad for being single, who would otherwise not have felt sad if society hadn't told them that they ought to be. More often than not, people are projecting their own fears of being alone onto single individuals. There are many, many people who have never learned who they are on their own, and so the idea of people who can be happy without a relationship is a bizarre concept.

Still, although I do feel that people can be happy and lead fulfilling lives without a relationship, I knew I had some psychological blocks which were preventing me from being successful romantically. This was a flaw that had become so because I was addicted, in a sense, to the maladaptive behaviour. I was addicted to feeling comfortable, and not allowing myself to be vulnerable.

Our brains crave such behaviours because they are often easier than doing the right thing. Running away and hiding is easier than standing your ground and fighting. Often enough, the path of least resistance is a bread-crumb trail of misguided behaviours, and so for me, making excuse after excuse to end a relationship was easier than becoming vulnerable and committed and open. It was also an easier path than addressing my own issues. As a result, my brain chose this easier avenue every single time and began to find relief and comfort in getting out of what felt like a trap, but it would have actually been good for me if I had stuck with the path which made me uncomfortable.

Perhaps the most frequent excuse I've made, or have heard made for me, is that I'll know for sure when I've met the right person. I'll somehow straighten up and sort my shit out the day I meet said person, as they descend from the clouds and into my life. Perhaps this is true, but it sounds to me like some romanticised notion of how these things play out. Life doesn't work like our favourite rom-coms. What is far more likely is that I've already met someone who would suit me perfectly, and I've passed them up as a result of this error in my code. This seems more probable than me becoming in some way aware that I'm in the presence of 'the one'. The existence of a perfect partner surely depends a great deal on our ability to be in a relationship. The one could have been someone I dated and ran away from out of fear. This seems more likely than being struck down with some transcendent knowledge upon meeting a particular person and suddenly becoming capable of committing. No person could solve my problems for me, and thinking in this way was just another method of ignoring the issue at hand.

In fact, I'm unbelievably confident I won't know at all, and the real concern will actually be that the realisation will hit me months or years later, at a time when it is far too late to act accordingly. I will be some older version of myself lamenting a happily married ex who I let go of because I was too afraid to face my flaws. That's a future I do not want. There is a good chance I have met someone already who is a suitable match and I was too concerned with ignoring my problems to understand this.

On the other hand, there's a case to be made for over-intellectualising all of this.

Applying an almost clinical version of rationale to something that is biologically driven may not make much sense. When you really get into things, it's difficult to know what is a problem, and what is an instinctual reaction. And so, although it feels like I'm making choices throughout my relationship history, I am possibly making explanations for decisions my brain has made without me. This is a pretty well-known tenant of free will theory. (Sam Harris talks about this frequently, and his books are quite good at explaining these complexities if you're into this sort of thing). I may not be in the driver seat at all. In a sense, I could have no control over what's happening and am only trying to make sense of things in which I have no control, post-hoc.

It's an important thing to consider, but when it comes down to it I feel like this line of thinking, even if true, only works to soothe an ego and make excuses for behaving badly. It still feels like I'm the one making destructive decisions so I need to treat the behaviour as such. I still feel the guilt and the loneliness and the shame in the aftermath, so even if I'm only along for the ride, it would be better for all involved if I could change the trajectory of the behaviour, and mitigate the emotional despair. Whether it be true or not, it *feels* like I'm the one making the decisions, so I should assume I am for the sake of my mental wellbeing.

In the heat of a humid July these thoughts took hold of my mind and I was sure to God that there was something wrong with me, whilst being equally sure that there was nothing wrong at all. It was a case of Schrodinger's Flaw, where the flaw existed, and didn't exist, depending on whether I chose to observe it or not. Notably, the flaw's hold on me strengthened or weakened depending on how good I felt about myself. On anxious days, I was the flawed, awful version of myself. On good days, I was simply looking out for myself and there was nothing wrong. The truth undoubtedly lay somewhere between these poles.

I had a casual-ish relationship for a few weeks towards the end of August. I think the age difference between us had set a precedent in my head that it would never amount to anything serious, so it ended after a few short weeks. I thought it had been fine, and she had to move to Dublin anyway. Still, it did feel like I was making excuses again, and when I talked to her weeks later after she told me she felt the end came out of nowhere for her, and I knew then that it always did. One day everything is fine, the next day I am explaining why things are no longer working for me. It always blindsides people, because there is rarely anything objectively wrong with the relationship. I am just running away. And this is where my variety of madness becomes a bit annoying for everyone.

See, I choose to run from relationships. I could be in one if I stuck it out and overcame the building fear. I could even be very happy in one if I kept my eyes focused on my own patch of grass. But I can't and so I'm not. I choose to be alone every time which suggest that I want to be alone. I take myself away from companionship and I sit alone in my room typing furious words at the world. And on these nights with the wind battering away and the rain crackling like fire overhead, I suffer from dreadful loneliness. A loneliness I have inflicted. A loneliness I could avoid if I liked myself enough to avoid it. A loneliness that wouldn't have to exist if I just gave a single person a chance. I sit in on these nights, trapped in the loneliness I have chosen. Although I wanted a relationship – something real – the stronger part of me would always run away. So I existed in this internal conflict of wanting to be with someone, yet not being able to.

If I'm not making a decision to address the issue, if I'm choosing to be alone and to allow loneliness to close in on me, then I have to conclude that I've never really loved myself. I've liked me in spurts, I've enjoyed the interesting parts, but have I wanted myself to be happy the way one ought to? Have I really wanted happiness for myself?

These questions flooded my head towards the end of that summer, as I lay awake looking up through the skylight in that little rented room. I could feel my heartbeat too prominently to get comfortable and I was wondering why the fuck I continued to do this to myself. It was an altogether strange time inside my head, but I'd made an important discovery, one that had never occurred to me before then. It felt as though this realisation was a beginning to getting better.

Romantic Notions

I began to resent the idea of meeting my potential future life-partner through an app on my phone. I began to pull back from even finding some sort of emotional oasis. I wasn't able to reciprocate one at that time, and I felt that using someone for emotional recourse without returning that favour was disingenuous. By the time my 26th birthday rolled around at the end of November, my hair was longer than it had ever been. I felt more alone than I ever had in my whole life, but this aloneness only manifested as loneliness some of the time, usually when I simultaneously inflicted it upon myself and framed myself as a victim of circumstance. When the self-pity came, the loneliness was hot on its heels.

Around this time I had an awfully romantic notion of who I was. I saw my isolation as some sort of important thing that had to happen in the story of my life. Just like in Dublin, I felt that my struggle was necessary for my work. I failed to see that my isolation was a choice I was making, and chose to see it as something that was simply happening to me. There was a part of me which believed that my writing would become terrible again if I addressed my loneliness, so all my attempts at improvement were half-arsed. Romantically, as I said above, I was in No Man's Land. I kept getting into situations where I'd be really into someone before we met, and they wouldn't seem too keen. Then when we did meet the roles essentially reversed, and I'd have to break it to them that it wasn't for me, even though a few days previous it definitely had been for me, and now they were more invested than I was.

I'd go from doing everything I could to change their minds about me, to no longer wanting to be with them. I can only imagine how this makes someone feel. It made for confusing conversations and understandable frustration. After several of these types of unnecessary situations I figured that maybe romance in the Covid-era wasn't going to work out for me. This was a decision I wrestled with, as my logical conclusion collided abrasively with my physical needs. I had been using relationships as means to physical ends, rather than seeing value in them beyond sex. Although not consciously decided, this was my view of relationships for years due to my emotional unavailability. The reasoning behind it is distorted, but it goes that if one doesn't wish to be hurt again after being deeply hurt, then relationships would not be a place for emotional vulnerability. And if you're not vulnerable in a relationship then all they can be is a means to an end, and at the expense of the other person's real feelings.

I spent the month of September deep-diving on Enlightenment philosophy, which inevitably led me to become fixated on the work of Immanuel Kant. I'm not going to lay out his whole thing here – mainly because I don't understand it all well enough to recount to you coherently – but one of his most famous ideas is *the Categorical Imperative*. To cut a long, long story short for you (and mostly likely butcher the actual meaning), this is the idea that human beings should never be used as a means to an end. We shouldn't use people as pawns in our grand schemes, morally speaking. For example, human lives shouldn't be sacrificed in order to save other lives. It's a sticky but important moral standpoint. And it's one that I came to relate to quite deeply.

When I got to a point where my biological urges clashed with the unlikely scenario of me finding a relationship in the second lockdown of a global pandemic, I began to think, in this specific and rare circumstance, that it was perfectly okay to use other people as a means to an end. Other people did this often, so why couldn't I? Other people seemed to easily have casual relationships, and without any internal conflict. I thought I could do the same. Later, I came to realise I was totally and utterly wrong, and my conscience would suffer the consequences of that. I was not built for casual sex, but my mind was also convinced that it was not built for a long-term relationship, either.

The Lesson

Before 2020, I thought I'd turned a corner. I thought I'd at least figured out a way to look beyond my emotional unavailability. I thought I might be ready to open up and lay myself bare to someone. I was dead wrong. If anything, I was as bad as I'd ever been. Which is why 2020 was important for me mentally. I went through a harsh battery of loneliness. There were some hard-to-swallow truths in those 12 months. It was a challenging time because I finally came to understand how monstrous I'd been for so long. I became aware of how deeply ingrained my unavailability was. I'd put up these massive fronts which didn't allow any vulnerability, and I framed not being in a relationship like I was a victim in all of it.

I often told myself running from a person was a good decision. But it wasn't a choice, it was a compulsion. I couldn't break through that fear of being hurt again, so I didn't allow myself to be in a relationship where I could be hurt, even if the reward was worth the risk.

When 2020 began I thought I'd cracked the code on my mental health. I thought I'd never struggle again. I was living more in the light than ever. I was doing my best to stay honest and learn how to not feel guilty all of the time. But this wasn't the case. I wasn't being entirely honest with myself. 2020 was such an important year for me, and for many others, because our mental health took such a hammering and we still got through it. As the year went on, and as I realised my mental health was far from perfect, I began to develop a more structured mental health routine. This allowed me to identify issues within me. Once this happened, I had all the time in the world to work on these problems, to try and understand what was causing them, and to ask myself the tough questions so that I could finally heal from my past.

It's not an easy thing to do, coming to terms with your flaws and your misdeeds. We tend to hide them from. We convince ourselves that we were acting in the best ways possible. But if we saw other people behaving how we have, we'd say they were bad people. I did that. I gave myself leeway. I rationalised bad behaviour, making other people the villain to make myself feel better.

In ways, and without minimising the destruction of that year, I'm grateful for 2020 because it allowed me to get to place where I could confront these problems and start to work on them. Was it painful? Absolutely. I had to swallow many bitter pills. A serious amount of them. Accepting that there are parts of you which you don't like can be heart-breaking, but it's worthwhile because it's only once you accept these things that you can start to like yourself again. The year 2020 brought me out of the darkness, where I was hiding from myself, and into the light, where I could stop feeling so anxious and guilty and ashamed of who I was, and of who I am.

Production Anxiety

Many anxieties have colonised my mind over the years, but none have had such a long and consistent reign as the anxiety and guilt associated with the pressure to be productive. Over the years my mother has been consistent in telling me that I need to go easy on myself. She's also a source of wisdom I have ignored more often than I should have. This pressure, it's the making and breaking of many of us. Guilt has always plagued my mind whenever I've spent time 'unproductively', and this is mainly because my definitions of productivity and success were so rigid and small-minded that any time spent outside of this zone has been considered wasteful. Productivity was only ever time spent working. It didn't include any other categories, even though downtime is required to be productive at all. If I spent time with friends, family, or trying to relax, my mind told me I was doing the wrong thing constantly. It made me feel bad for taking breaks. To mitigate this, I would cave in to the voice and quieten it with work. This subsequently caused any time spent doing what was once enjoyable work to become burdensome and torturous, because I was enslaved to the notion that I had to be productive. It also made fun feel blunted because there was always a cloud of pressure hanging over me. Guilt, pressure and stress accompanied every moment away from the work.

There is no productivity to be found in time spent doing things that make us feel bad. This is not to say all of our time should be spent pursuing pleasure or fun, either. I mean that our work, if we are passionate about it, should bring us a certain level of satisfaction. It shouldn't make us feel bad when we spend time away from it, either. When you constantly feel a pressure to be working, then nothing you work on gives you any joy – the work is forced and difficult, whilst the time spent away from the work is stressful because you feel you should be working. You can hardly call this productive, or successful. When our passion becomes the root of our misery, because of the pressure we put on ourselves, there is nothing to gain from it, and so this is not productivity – it's torture. You should want to keep going with your work, but it shouldn't enslave you. That's what has been the case for me, and although a lot of work gets done, there is a constant level of stress all day every day, no matter what I'm doing.

This experience has been so common to my life, that for a long time I didn't know I was under pressure or stressed, because these feelings were my default day-to-day experience. It's like a noise that initially bothers you but after some time you can no longer even hear. You learn to block it out because it doesn't look like it's going away. It's only when you get a moment's silence that you realise how loud it has been I have no doubt that you've felt similarly at times throughout your own life. Production anxiety is a bastard, maybe the most consistent bastard going. During 2020 and 2021 this particular anxiety ruled over my mind like never before.

Scattered and Unfocused

Nothing was working out. Nothing could work out the way I was going at it – half-arsed as always. I appeared to be busy, and I was, but I was scattered and unfocused. Too many ambitions were getting less than the attention required to make them come into being. There were times where I was stretched too thinly, meaning I was never putting my entire focus on a single goal. I never put enough work into anything for it to become something exceptional or worthwhile. Too many fingers in too many pies is the expression you might use. It was chaos, and I don't really know how I managed to get anything done.

This was across the board.

These half measures happened with everything. I was like a dog chasing multiple balls at the same time. I wanted all of them, but only had the ability to carry one properly. If I was meant to be editing I was writing poems. If I was meant to be writing a story I was partying with friends. If I was meant to be working then I was querying agents. I was always doing something but it never seemed to be the thing I ought to do.

Everything led somewhere good if I could only throw myself in fully, but I could never put myself fully into a single thing. There was a point where I was working full time, writing a book, playing national level basketball and running a mental health blog all at the same time. I was burning the candle from every angle you can imagine. I was altogether too impulsive, rather than being single-minded about one worthwhile goal. I was working hard but I was nowhere near focused. The difference is important.

This sort of malfunction seeped into all parts of what you might call life. I could never really socialise well because I felt the all too familiar productivity guilt giving me grief for not working. When I did escape my social obligations to work, I'd work hard, but rarely on the one thing I ought to have worked on. I'd see a new opportunity and pounce on it, thus leaving whatever I was working on to settle in the wayside. As I worked more I'd also lament my lack of social life – the social life I abandoned by choice to get more work done. The sickness touched everything. It's a loop of anxiety – I'd be anxious that I wasn't working when I was with friends, and then I'd be anxious about not having enough of a social life when I was working. Around and around I went in this sort of chaotic cycle without an inclination of how to fix it because, well, I reckoned that's just how I was. It felt more like reality than an actual problem for a long time. It felt like I just had to put up with these feelings instead of finding a way to resolve them. I figured everyone felt the same and was just hiding it well. I didn't understand the way I was feeling to be any bit abnormal, and so I never questioned if there might be another way to feel.

The jealousy I felt towards other people, and in particular, other writers, began to become more and more intense, too, especially in 2020. There was a stage where it got so bad that I actually got frustrated by a character on a TV show (specifically, Nick from *New Girl*) because he landed a big publishing deal, which still eluded me. The pressure I put on myself was so severe that even fictional characters getting deals made me feel like I was failing. I talked a big game about staying in your own lane but I was addicted to peering over the walls into the lanes of other, perceivably more successful people.

My value was totally dependent on my position in relation to other writers. On days when I felt I was 'successful' and ahead of the pack I felt good, and when I felt like I was failing in comparison, I felt awful. My definition of success, and my mechanism for quantifying success were misguided. I thought personal success was something that was supposed to make other people feel inferior, because this is how other people's success made me feel. Instead of viewing success as happiness, or contentment, it was shrouded by superficial validation, newspaper articles, and vanity. I wanted to be well known for a long time, and this made me miserable. It made the landscape of my inner world significantly more toxic than it needed to be, and I was totally complicit.

The need for this distorted success plagued me, and it made me feel guilty for not being productive all of the time.

I've felt the guilt of productivity hang over me like a cloud for most of my adult life – this constant pressure to be tipping away at something. It's a persistent niggle in the back of the head. We all get it at times, I'm sure. It's the voice that told you that you should have been studying when you weren't back in your school days. It's the voice that tells you to get back to work when you're chatting by the coffee machine in the office. This voice will give it a rest when you feel you've done enough work for the day, but if you don't do enough, it's a loud alarm that won't turn off. This voice is necessary at times undoubtedly. It's the voice of ambition, and it's the reason anyone gets anything worthwhile done.

For me, the problem is that this voice has been given a megaphone and an unlimited supply of caffeine. It's relentless.

This voice has stopped me from enjoying things across the board – things that I would enjoy if it weren't for that voice telling me I wasn't working hard enough. My mind is always thinking about work to some degree. I've been half-present around family and friends, at events, on dates, holidays – every aspect of my life is affected. Trying to relax has been difficult, historically. I feel guilty for giving myself much needed breaks. I can't even watch TV without forcing myself to ignore the burning urge to go and do some work. Whether it's cleaning, or working out, or writing, my mind has always demanded that I do those things rather than activities for the pure sake of enjoyment. And I've always thought it was something everyone battled with to the same degree, but I was wrong about that.

Other people can switch off the pressure. They can flip a switch and not think about work again until it is time to do more work. I, on the other hand, feel bad every minute I'm not doing any work.

The nature of my work means it will never be done. There is always something to write, after all. This means that the productivity anxiety will theoretically never fully cease, because there is always something I could be working on. There is always something that could hang over me if I allow it, and I usually let it take full control, because I am too insecure about my writing. Because of this, I have feel I have to always be writing if I am to become 'successful' enough to be satisfied, and thus, to stop putting pressure on myself. You can see how little sense it makes. But therein lies the real issue – my idea of happiness has been tied up with this misled definition of success. It ensures that I will never be happy, because even if I do achieve this 'success', the goalposts will undoubtedly move, and I'll be left unsatisfied until I accomplish the next thing, and then the next thing, and so on.

Of course, what is really happening here is a lack of discipline.

Up until now I wasn't able to compartmentalise my time and so every minute was given to everything rather than focusing on a singular task. I'd bounce between things all day rather than setting aside time for each specific goal. It's an adlibbed balancing act rather than organised engagement. There was no time set aside for downtime either because I was undisciplined. I was constantly thinking about something without allowing myself any breaks. I wasn't able to switch off. All of my time was to be used in some sort of productive way with no real idea or rules about how this might look. It made me quite antsy. There have been very few times where I've been totally unstressed about taking a day off. Days where I have been okay with not working have come sparingly and have never lasted very long.

I've always been the type that needs to start working on something as soon as it's assigned. I'm also the type that needs to reply to text messages as soon as they come in, or do a task as soon as I become aware that it needs doing. You can rest assured knowing that your email will be read and responded to as soon as I know it exists. It is only quite recently in my life that I understood these behaviours to be anxiety-driven. Whether it was a college essay or just some non-urgent form the bank needed, as soon as it landed on my desk it had to be done in that moment. I find it very difficult to put things off, or to prioritise one thing over another.

That's what anxiety is. It's the inability to ignore your phone when it vibrates. If I know a notification has come in then I have to respond to it immediately or it will remain on my mind until a time where I can respond to it. I become totally distracted until I have scratched this itch. I cannot relax from the moment a thing needs doing until the moment the thing is done. You'll rarely find me forgetting to do something because once it's assigned to my mind I can't unassign it. There will be no level of peace until the task is done. This works in my favour at times of course, because the anxiety beckons me to work more often so that I feel it less. It forces me to sit down and do the work just so I can feel some sort of relief at the end of the day. Knowing that progress has been made, that I at least got some words down during the day brings with it a sense of satisfaction, and thus, a sense of relief. I'm sure you can relate to that. Knowing you got all of what you needed to get done for the day can be quite fulfilling. List made – tasks ticked off. That's a universal good time.

However, in far more ways, this production anxiety works against me. It makes me sacrifice time with friends, family and romantic partners to appease the voice telling me to work. I begin to feel bad when I'm not working and this in turn causes me to frame any time spent away from the work as time wasted. It makes me reluctant to sacrifice any time to anything I haven't subconsciously deemed 'productive'. It has warped my sense of value to think of everything in terms of productivity.

I have been reluctant to give my time to anyone else. Imagine having a boyfriend or girlfriend, who thinks spending time with you this weekend isn't their most productive use of time. They spend time because they *have to* rather than because they *want to*. And every minute they are with you, there is a part of them churning away about the work they think they should be doing. Imagine having a friend who is only friends with you on their terms, and when it suits their schedule. The person who makes you feel like you are constantly second priority is an asshole. I was that asshole for a long time but I thought it was justifiable in some way. I figured it would all eventually be worthwhile. I thought the ends justified the means, and I didn't stop to think about how my perspective on productivity was slowly making me miserable.

Admitting to myself that I have been this asshole was hard. It takes a lot of work and self-awareness to not be that asshole because the productivity anxiety doesn't just disappear. It's still here. I just have to learn to harness it.

Production anxiety can be a useful tool if you learn to control it. It can make you productive in the times you need to be productive. With some discipline and a little bit of organisation, you can make this pressure to be productive, well, productive. I remember having a drunk conversation with my brother one Spring evening about this. He told me that the problem was less about anxiety as it was about time management. You may not be able to tame the anxiety but you can cage it. Setting time aside to listen to this voice each day makes sense. Having a schedule where I know what hours are available for writing, and what hours are available for downtime, leisure, exercise etc. makes far more sense than what I was doing. An average day for me would consist of doing little bits of everything with no evident structure – I'd write a few hundred words and then I'd read a few pages of a book, and then I'd learn some Spanish, and then I'd come back to the manuscript, and then I'd write a poem. I was all over the place and it was **this** that was making me anxious more than anything else. It wasn't so much the work as it was my approach to it. There was no sense of progress. It felt chaotic and that made me feel uncomfortable.

Once this became clear to me, and I sorted out a schedule, things became much more manageable. I started getting up before my day job started to do the work I felt was most urgent, and then I'd set more time aside in the evening to address the less urgent work. The production anxiety didn't go away, and it probably never will, but it has become quieter. It has been tamed. I gave it a space to roam free rather than allowing it to dominate my mind. Now, I work in the hours set aside for working, and I forget about it when they're over. This allows me to be present with my friends and family, and it allows me to actually enjoy things like movies, or exercise, or whatever it may be. This specific anxiety was a wild animal inside my head and now it been checked to some degree.

The Lesson

Production anxiety is not so much the most detrimental of anxieties for me as it is the most consistent. It doesn't cause me to spiral into serious mental health problems, but it can put me in a constant state of stress and agitation. It is the one anxiety I have known to always be there, lurking below the surface. Even before I was introduced to the idea of mental health. I've always feel the guilt it causes. The problem with this form of anxiety is that it's a gateway issue to more affective problems like imposter syndrome, and more pressingly, an inability to be happy.

If you never concede that you are in fact doing enough to deserve happiness, then you will never accept that you are worthy of said happiness. This production guilt is almost a happiness blocker. It surrounds your happiness and tells you that you're not allowed access to it until you've done more work. The problem is there is not enough work to satisfy this monster. The secret to getting around this is so simple that I overlooked it until recently – you can do your work *and* be happy simultaneously, I just didn't know that to be true.

The Fear of Death

Pope John Paul II died when I was eleven. I didn't know him personally, obviously, but his death had me scrambling for answers.

The death of the pope brought about my first real experience with death anxiety. It wasn't so much that I was sad that a 80-something year-old I'd never met had died. It was more that I knew then that the jig was up. I'm not religious at all now, but I was to a point back then just because I didn't know any better. I'd been raised Catholic and there was no critical-thought capacity instilled in my mind yet, so I assumed what I had been raised on was just the way things were. I went to mass and I whispered prayers to myself before bed and I felt bad for existing – the usual Catholic vibe.

When the pope died, the curtain fell, and I knew I was fucked. The pope dying confirmed that I could never be immortal and would one day die, too. It confirmed that the people in my life – my family, my friends – would also fail to escape. This might sound funny but back then, I wasn't so certain that I'd definitely eventually have to die. If the alleged best friend of God can die, then what hope did I have for escaping it? I ran into my parents' bedroom in the middle of the same night crying, because of this fear of death. I couldn't make sense of it. I realised then, maybe for the first time, that one day I was going to die – one day I would no longer exist and that scared me. It scared me right down to the core of my soul, the part you can't really feel unless you are in serious danger.

Even at this young age I had a sense that there's nothing for us after death. The idea of heaven seemed too good to be true. It also didn't make sense to me that you'd live, only to die, only to start living again. In my gut I could feel it was just endless nothingness for eternity once you kick it. That's an uncomfortable thing to consider as an adult let alone as a child. It's scary. It can cause panic and terror to bubble up in the throat like vomit. Death has always been a fascination of mine, not in the sense of admiration, like a favourite sports team, but more so like how people are compelled by hearing bad news, or love to watch murder documentaries. We are simultaneously enamoured by death yet avoid thinking about our own demise. Our whole lives are designed to stop ourselves from thinking about dying. No matter who you are or what you do, you don't know for certain what happens after you die. And this is probably why people avoid thinking about it, or talking about it, because it causes us to face up to our fears without getting any sort of closure. I've been fascinated by what happens after death because it's unknowable, which makes it uniquely rare in this universe of ours.

When I try to broach the subject of death, and this usually happens after a few pints, it's a topic of conversation avoided by the more sensible among us, perhaps. We tend to construct our entire lives in an attempt to stay far away from any lingering thoughts of our own mortality. We don't want to talk about death, yet we are the only animal on this planet with the ability to even comprehend it. We walk around every day, doing whatever we can to extend our lives, trying to avoid thinking about our imminent demise.

We're the only species that does this because we're the only species that knows that it will one day die. Dogs don't have panic attacks caused by thoughts about not existing. We have a temporal capacity to consider the future, but this comes at the price of being able to look beyond ourselves into a world in which we no longer exist. It seems remiss to have this ability yet be terrified to use it. Because thinking of death, despite how scary it can be, grounds us in the present.

For most of my life I've avoided these thoughts of death, and so, when they eventually do consume me, they cause severe anxiety and panic. When these dreaded thoughts roll back around, all I can think about for long weeks is not existing and all I feel is dread and deep-rooted fear.

This is a less than ideal way to exist – avoiding thinking about an entire aspect of life out of fear, yet feeling truly awful when you inevitably find yourself thinking about it. How do we find a way to get around this anxiety? Well, the Stoics reckon that you need to think about death (Or whatever your fear is) more often than you currently do. It's almost like exposure therapy, to desensitise oneself, but it's more than that – it's coming to terms with death, and understanding that it can't be scary because it's unavoidable. You don't fear sleep, or being born, yet these are unavoidable parts of life too.

We have been given an ability to conceptualise our own mortality, and I'd like to believe that it's not solely in our wheelhouse just to induce fear. We should possibly only fear things that we could have avoided if we behaved differently. We should fear car crashes and falling from cliff edges and shifting the wrong people, because we can actually prevent these things from happening to a degree. We can't however, prevent being dead. Therefore, we could rationally fear dying by a specific means, like in a car crash, or falling from a cliff, because these means of death can be avoided. But we can't prevent actually dying. Therefore we shouldn't fear actually being **dead**, because that is neither avoidable nor optional. It is something which happens to everyone without exception.

This is fine in theory, but death can still be a formidable thing to think about if you don't find a way to come to terms with it. It's still quite scary if you can't find a way to accept it.

Death-Induced Panic Attacks

During the summer of 2020, I was spending a decent amount of time around the beaches of Cork – Garryvoe, Myrtleville, Garrettstown – and in particular Ballycotton, which wasn't exactly close to where I lived. A short 35 minute drive got me there, and I spent the evenings either jumping from the pier with some friends or walking the cliff walk to try and find a ship that had washed up there months previous (it's easy to find considering it isn't hidden and is sign-posted). The July-August-September of that year were remarkably warm, and the water in Ireland could actually be used as a means to cool oneself down instead of turning one into an icicle, which is as rare a thing as you can imagine on an island famous for its cold rains in the middle of the Atlantic Ocean.

The summer of 2020 was a mixed bag for me, as it also brought with it panic attacks, mainly triggered by a primal fear of death. Fear of death is the most human fear you can have because it is an exclusively human fear. If you want to, you can imagine what it might be like to not exist whatsoever.

As I grew older and learned more, this fear became worse and began to inspire my mind to shut down. It would cause me to have long, sleepless nights, as my mind's eye was a moth to the terrible flame of death. When the fear becomes too severe I can have intense panic attacks. These attacks don't happen too often, but every few months or so I'll be stricken down with thoughts attracted to this idea of not existing. The thought of not existing is like a bad smell, one that you detest but can't stop yourself from smelling again, becoming disgusted each time you do. These thoughts can result in the offset of these deep-rooted panic attacks, the outcomes of which leave me unsettled for days, and sometimes weeks after.

Ernest Becker's book *The Denial of Death* talks a lot about why we tend to avoid thinking about death. We build great distracting lives to stop ourselves from using this ability to understand death, which suggests that being able to conceptualise death is more of a bad side effect of evolution than it is a positive attribute of it. I've read extensively about how philosophers throughout the ages, like Freud and Camus, could never escape their death anxiety. Despite their great intellect, not even they could figure out death because there is no way to be certain of what lies beyond – our ideas on death are based in faith entirely.

Death, seems to me, to be the root of all our actions. Our fear of death comes about by living, and we fill our lives with distractions and noise to drown out that fear. Even this book is a result of that fear at the base level. We all crave a sense of immortality, despite how unlikely it is, and despite how egotistical it makes us sound. Books, legacies, achievements, even children – all of these pursuits are an attempt to escape the clutches of death.

In order to mitigate this fear then, we create elaborate dramas to distract ourselves with. We create societies and jobs and politics and families and everything else you can think of in an attempt to outrun our imminent mortality. We can reasonably trace all of our actions back to a fear of death. And yet, although death, and the fear of it, are the primary source of our suffering, they're also the primary motivator for our progress.

Knowing that the inevitability of death is looming causes us to try and make our lives meaningful. It causes us to look forward, to live beyond our time and ourselves. It motivates us to elongate our lives, to pass on our genetic heritage, to do things we'd not be bothered to do if we had unlimited time. Death is our primary fear, but also our primary muse. All of our passions would be stamped out if we lived forever – it is the temporary aspect of our existence that drives us on. I've often wondered whether a person who has lived life well fears death in the end. I like to believe they don't, at least not to the same extent as the person who lives a half-life, and avoids thoughts of death for their entire lives.

That being said, the fear of death still causes terror in me. Although I can understand the intellectual arguments for why we need not fear death, I still find it difficult to separate from the emotional turmoil these thoughts cause within me. When I really delve into the reality of death, and what it means for me, it causes deep and severe anxiety, as well as panic and terror. This is mainly because, like I mentioned earlier, I think there is nothing when we die.

I have tried to make a habit of forcing myself to think about this fact often, though, because although it causes me to suffer, it also brings about a more grateful mindset in the aftermath. If we are conscious of the fact that life can be taken at any moment, it allows us to become more grateful in the present. We tend to stop worrying about things, which are at their core, arbitrary, and we focus more on the immediate and genuine aspects of our existence. Being aware of death allows us to acknowledge what is of genuine importance. This may be why people don't fuss over frivolous things around funerals, because death is at the forefront of our minds.

Gratitude for life emerges from the fear of death, and I think there's something worthwhile and important in that. It's a suffering worth enduring, because we become grateful for things which are otherwise taken for granted. We no longer care about being cut off in traffic, or working long hours, or any of the would-be grievances which can cause distress. We shouldn't live completely castrated by this fear of death. Although it can be difficult in the beginning to force yourself to think about the concept of death, you can use it to enrich your life. Our lives have meaning because of their impermanence. We can reach fulfilment exactly because we must eventually die. If life went on forever then nothing we ever do would mean anything, because we'd quite literally have all the time in the world. There'd be no endeavour worth taking because with unlimited time and enough motivation, we could accomplish everything. There's no meaning found in an infinite life. Meaning is to be found in the fact that our lives end, and so living with knowledge of this end allows us to hold onto a sense of purpose. It allows us to live for something.

I came to this understanding through reading on the subject, but mainly through experience of intense panic attacks as a result of this fear. I realised that thoughts about death are unavoidable, and will happen from time to time, so living in fear of them was doing more damage than good. I was leaving myself open to panic attacks because I was afraid of these thoughts. Whatever way I looked at it, the fear of death was going to remain, but it needn't have to cause me such intense terror every time it came up. I didn't have to be shaken to my core. Something had to change. It was either try and overcome the fear, or drive on in spite of it. After the last panic attack – arguably the worst one – there was no longer any room to live in fear of something that's unavoidable.

At the start of the pandemic, before I moved out to the house in Douglas, I had a panic attack about death in my childhood bedroom. It was a lovely summer's day as far as I remember. The sun crept in through the windows of my parents' home in thick golden brushstrokes. I was working as a linguist at the time, and like many people, our work was being conducted from home due to the virus. It's easy to find yourself distracted in these situations, especially once the novelty of a new schedule diminishes into normality.

Often, when I work I put on a podcast for background noise. Don't we all? Usually it's something light, a comedian talking shite or something. On this occasion though, I decided upon Russell Brand and Ricky Gervais – the former a passionate spiritualist, and the latter an avid atheist. The subject matter that could potentially arise enticed me, but it also meant we could wander into more terror-inducing territory. I don't remember the specifics of their conversation, but they got to a point where they were discussing death, and Gervais was going on about how he was adamant that we rot in the ground after we die, that we cease to exist. There is no afterlife to him. There is no consciousness beyond. There is nothing.

And this little perspective is all it took on this particular day for me to erupt into a debilitating panics attack. What Gervais was alluding to is something I feel in my bones to be true too already, but this common knowledge hardly makes that thought of it any easier, especially when you spend your whole life avoiding thinking about such things. Knowing that an uncomfortable thing is true does not make it any less uncomfortable, it just makes it real.

Importantly, for anyone who reads that and thinks I'm just pulling the truth of it from nowhere, what I really mean is that I know it to be true for me. The idea of there being nothing after death makes more sense to me than the idea of an afterlife does, but obviously I don't know for sure – nobody knows for sure. It's a gut feeling, and it could easily be totally wrong. I'd be overjoyed if it was wrong, really. However, for me, an afterlife is something akin to Santa Claus for adults, in that, we get rewarded at the end of life for good behaviour. I just don't buy it – it makes little logical sense that one would die only to live again. If this is true, what on Earth is the point of death, and limited time, and decaying, at all? Maybe it's not a logical thing, though, which is why people have their faith. You have to take a chance to believe in an afterlife, and I suppose this just isn't a chance I've ever been willing to take.

I understand why one might want to believe in an afterlife. It's both enticing and optimistic. The idea of there being something is far less scary than a reality where there is nothing, and I'd wager many people turn to religious ideas of an afterlife, not so much out of adamant belief, but out of deep-rooted fear of no longer existing.

To contextualise my mental state prior to the panic attack, I was already anxious. My trip to South America had been cancelled and I was feeling quite lost. For the first time in a long while I had no specific long-term goal. I didn't know what to do with myself. When this happens to me I begin to feel stagnant, like I'm not working towards anything worthwhile, and this often expresses itself as anxiety. The idea of floating without an aim has always felt like disempowerment above all else – if you're not moving forward, you're moving backwards. In this state, I start believing that I should make drastic changes in my life – start a different career, go back to college, move abroad – that kind of thing. So I was already on edge during this time in 2020. I was already in a place where my mental health wasn't in peak condition.

I was also one day removed from a hangover, so the usual remnants of fear clambered around my mind like lost children. I'd overdone it on the Saturday night during a Zoom quiz, and the hangover had bled into a second day. Finally, we were in the middle of a pandemic. Notions of death and despair were already laid on thick. There was no sense of certainty about anything and this painted a new layer of anxiety across the entire world. In sum, I was in a strange mental health-stalemate, not unhappy, but not flourishing (This is called languishing) and I was also taking on the brutal attack of self-contempt which comes hand-in-hand with a hangover. Basically, I was primed to be tipped over the edge, and Ricky Gervais' take on the afterlife, or lack thereof, is all it took.

As the reality of not existing became firm in the front of my mind once again, I began to panic in a very intense way. Panic attacks are strange, and difficult to explain to someone who's never experienced one. It feels like you're in a very dangerous situation when there is absolutely no physical threat. Your body goes into fight or flight mode when there is no rational or obvious reason to. There's an adrenaline spike, your heartrate rockets, and you feel like something is about to explode. If you're afraid of spiders imagine what it would feel like if hundreds of them were crawling all over you, and there was nothing you could do to stop it. That's how my experience of panic attacks has always felt. Fear takes over and it's very difficult to shake yourself out of.

When I began to panic, my breathing got away from me quickly, and I could feel my heartrate climbing through my ears. Being able to hear my own pulse generally tells me something is going wrong, particularly when I'm not exerting myself whatsoever. I suddenly felt trapped and claustrophobic, and my vision became warped and unfocused. The room I had in my parents' house is quite big, but no space would have been big enough then. There was sweat pooling on my forehead as well as my lower back, and it felt like my chest was caving in. I couldn't suck the air in fast enough. I knew early doors that what I was experiencing was a panic attack, so I pushed myself away from my desk using the wheels of my office chair, and I began to force big gulps of air into my lungs. I shoved my head in between my legs and held on for dear life. My brain was going a mile a minute, informing me that I was going to die, and when I did die I was going to stop existing, and that this would all come to fruition quite soon. It was relentless and repetitive and awful. In a sense, this particular attack was self-confirming which made it more difficult to disarm.

All while this was happening my parents were in the kitchen, oblivious to what was happening down the hall. I was too embarrassed to call for help, and despite all the work I've done on talking openly about mental health, was still self-stigmatising. I felt ashamed that I was having this attack, and believed there was something wrong with me for having it. I felt weak, and so I didn't say a word to anyone. Even as I write these words, the anxiety is brooding in the far reaches of my mind. Inklings of that existential doom are always there, the thoughts I used to try and keep at bay as much as possible.

Back in my room, I kept my head down as low as I could to get blood back into my brain, and after a lot of sweat and heavy breathing and some very long minutes – which felt like hours – I eventually came out of the panic spiral. I was depleted of all energy and drenched in cold sweat, so I changed my t-shirt, got some water and tried to force what had just happened from my mind. I went back to work and I pretended like all was fine when I emerged from the room an hour later.

If I'm honest with you, and I may as well continue to be, the attacks that come from the fear of death are rarely the worst part about the experience. In the moment they feel devastating, but it's the lingering doom that's the worst of all of it. The awareness of death doesn't just disappear once the attack ends. If anything the thoughts intensify. The weeks that followed this incident were far worse than the momentary attack, because I couldn't think about much else aside from death and the idea of not existing. It consumed me for days on end and I spent long nights awake deep into the early morning, only falling asleep a few short hours before the alarm went off.

I was constantly worrying about the inevitability of it all. It felt like I couldn't escape from the dread which death induced. The realisation of not existing brought fresh waves of fear each time it appeared on my mind's horizon. I'd try to imagine what it might be like to not exist at all and this would send fresh jolts of terror down my spine like volts of electricity. And these thoughts were addictive.

I couldn't keep myself away from them. Initially it made me feel like everything I was doing or trying to accomplish was frivolous – if I were going to cease existing eventually what was even the point in trying?

These experiences aren't at all pleasant, and quite frankly, I have suffered them mostly in silent solitude. It can be upsetting to know that thoughts alone can cause you to freeze up and feel like you're quite literally dying. I knew well enough the time would pass and I'd get through it because I'd been there before, but it doesn't make this experience any less unpleasant.

What's important is this – a few weeks after such an episode, when the lingering doom dissipates, I'm usually left with an appreciation for how bizarre it is to even be alive in this moment, using my body and mind and hands to reflect on the notion of not existing at all. These panic attacks over death encourage gratitude for the most mundane aspects of being alive. I remember sitting at my desk, being fascinated that I could even move my hands and arms using my mind. The thought that I was alive and breathing was encapsulating, and it made my evening runs in the summer sun feel euphoric, as I gazed out upon the world – the world that needn't exist at all – and marvelled at the fact that I somehow exist within it, too. It was me and the world, both existing despite the odds.

These death-anxiety panic attacks are truly awful, but they do leave you with an appreciation for how unlikely life is – how unlikely it is for us to be alive and be able to attach some sort of meaning to it despite our lack of knowledge and understanding. We are alive, and there is no clear reason why that should even be possible.

And it's this component of death anxiety that can be hijacked and used to enrich our lives. If we can live in a way where we are always somewhat aware of our eventual death, it can breed gratitude in the present. Suddenly, mundane things are tolerable and beautiful because the idea of being alive at all is so extraordinary. When we understand life to be totally unlikely and mind-blowing, everything within it carries a little bit of that awe. Even being able to type words on a computer and understand that these words came from a brain which evolved over millennia becomes this miraculous conception, and it's usually overlooked.

Sadly, this feeling doesn't last very long if you are avoiding thinking about death.

As the memories of the panic attack diminish, and the thoughts of death are pushed away by the intricacies of modern life, my appreciation for this life falls away too, as I have to 'get on with it'. The characteristics of modern life which we've built to distract us from the idea of death begin to do their job again, and suddenly I'm consumed by all the arbitrary worries and considerations exclusive to human beings. (Have you ever considered that we are the only animal on Earth which has to physically pay to be here?)

That being said, I've been left with a permanent feeling that the way I have been living is not how I ought to be, and I knew from then, with some certainty, that I needed to get out of the town in which I was born. The same one I'd lived in my whole life. I realised that there's more to life than chasing pleasure, there's more to life than careers and owning houses and the day-in, day-out we give so many hours to. We spend so much of our time doing things we don't find worthwhile just to have money we refuse to spend.

I don't know what this 'more' is, but I know it's out there. Death-anxiety has taught me that much. When you truly understand and consider how fleeting life is, and how easily it is taken from us, you might become hyper-aware that the way you are currently living is not one conducive with gratitude. You might find that you have been living a half-life, and that you've only been half-awake this whole time. We only live for a fleeting moment, but so many of us live as though we'll be here forever. We settle for less than we deserve because we refuse to acknowledge our own mortality. And yet, if we did face up to this truth, we'd live far better, because we'd always understand that no time is promised to us.

I began to see that I had spent many years of my young life asleep at the wheel. I was on autopilot, and it felt like I had only recently woken up. It's impossible to say when exactly it happened, but I imagine going through the trauma of losing my best friend to suicide shook me out to some degree. This realisation is also just a part of growing too. For example, if you've ever looked back at texts you sent from years ago and don't recognise the person, you'll have an understanding of this growth. It sometimes feels like you don't really know yourself, and that can be strange. It can feel like there are chunks of your life where you – the current you – weren't really present for. And in a way you weren't, because you haven't always been the current version of you. That only happened quite recently, and will last only briefly.

My awareness of death has brought me to life in a way, and I realise now how much time I have spent not thinking for myself at all. Instead, I just did what was done, or what everyone else was doing, and I rarely considered the consequences of my behaviour. It's so easy to fall into this pattern of just going along with things, rather than understanding your place within it all. It's less taxing mentally to go with the crowd, and of course sometimes it is the better course of action. However, living this way constantly isn't synonymous with truly living because you are not paving your own way – you're living someone else's version of your life. We have been gifted with an intelligence, a frontal lobe with which to try and understand ourselves. This is unique to humans, so it would be unwise if we neglected to use it.

You might wonder how many people still function in this mind-state, switched off, often only aware of, and interested in non-meaningful things, like celebrity culture, and Instagram, and looking a certain way, and partying – artificial things – but without any real grasp on what it means to be a human in the grand scheme of nature. Most of us have no inclination, and no desire to know more about what we are. This is what I mean by being asleep. There's a lack of thinking in some stratus of the modern era. We'd rather chase thrill than live well. We'd rather look a certain way than be a certain way. We'd rather have fun than have an impact. There is no ambition for more, because on some level we don't fully grasp how fleeting our lives are.

As a result, we are content to waste years of our lives working meaningless jobs to make money to buy things we'd never need and we call this living. But this isn't living – it's consumerism. It's being told what to do, but feeling like you're making decisions. That isn't life, at least not in a vast and full sense, and towards the end of the summer of 2020 I began to see this in a whole new light.

Becoming aware of being on autopilot is fine once you've been through something that forces you to take a hold of the wheel. I'm sure people with addictions and people with alcohol issues, and survivors of cataclysmic events can speak to that. On the other hand, your brain might protect itself from being shaken loose if you've not been through any sort of ordeal. If you're on autopilot your brain probably won't wish to be taken off of it. Autopilot is easy. You've lived a certain way your whole life and now you're being told it's wrong. Of course, you don't want to hear that. It's the path of least resistance, to live without challenging your beliefs, or what you consider to be important. It was much easier for me to avoid thoughts of death than it was to face up to them. It was more comfortable, but this doesn't mean it was the correct way to live.

You don't have to be burdened by the weight of reality when you're cruising. You don't need to know the why or the how. You can just happily march to your job, and march home, and watch TV and drink, and make-believe online, and live within the lie that you are acting freely. If you are acting freely, is the life you lead now the life you would really choose? I know what my answer is. The fact is, one day we all wake up and understand that we have wasted time on things that hold no significance. I imagine it is far better to realise this now, while you are still young, and while you still have time.

These insights come at the cost of comfort. They come with the price of knowing that how I was living was not conducive with fulfilment. Doing everything in half measures, without taking any real meaning from what you are doing is just as bad as living for aesthetic reasons, because there is no purpose in it. So, the understanding I came to about death and how to live contrasted starkly with how I was living. I was going on like I had all the time in the world, when I don't.

At the same time as this realisation, I was still making bad decisions when it came to my personal life. Although I knew I was treating some people poorly, it seemed almost impossible to stop. In this aspect I was still on autopilot, even though I was acutely aware of it. I just couldn't figure out how to switch it off.

The Lesson

Death anxiety has been a component of my mental life since I can remember. As I mentioned at the beginning of this essay, I remember crying to my parents in the middle of the night when it dawned on me that we may not exist after death. It's a scary thought and it would be disingenuous of me to say it's not. However, I have framed this fear negatively for most of my life. I've let it control me. I was scared to even go there in my mind. I wouldn't face up to it and this has caused me to have panic attacks in the past. But, after each one, I'm left with more gratitude for my life than I had before. I appreciate things more deeply. I actively engage in the time I spend with people, because now I fully grasp that eventually, the time I spend with a person will be the very last time.

Although it's scary, the good far outweighs the bad. This fear of death is a good thing now. It reminds me that nothing lasts forever. It gives meaning to things that would have none if I were immortal. It humbles us, and it makes us take stock of what we already have, rather than yearning for that which we desire.

Death comes for us all, and so it gives us all the opportunity to make our lives meaningful. Once you have your meaning and your purpose, that's when life begins.

The Lies We Tell Online

I fluctuated a lot in 2020, mentally, like. I was reluctant to admit anything was wrong while it went on. There were certainly issues which had been so finely tuned that I had come to see them as my personality. I suppose that's common enough – framing problems as quirks. Certain elements that could be improved were written off as 'immutable character traits,' which is a nifty cop out. Take for instance what we discussed earlier, the fact that once I got with a partner then I started wanting someone else as soon as things got real. This happened nearly every time. This 'grass is always greener' thinking had always been put down as an unchangeable trait in my head. *That's just how I am* – I'd tell myself that a lot.

In reality, it was a convoluted defence mechanism to stop myself from getting hurt, which only worked to hurt other people in the process. If I didn't get attached, I couldn't be hurt emotionally. It's like radical stoicism, and it's harmful. However, defence mechanisms aren't useful, nor actually defensive, if they indirectly hurt other people. In general, I went from happy to sad, solemn to lonely, content to anxious, quite frequently throughout the year. It was hard to string a few consistent days together, and it was frustrating to have a good day followed by a very anxious one. That was partly because I felt I wasn't in control of things due to the pandemic. The lack of control butted heads with my compulsion to be in control. Every day felt the same as the last, but the emotions were all over the place.

I felt I wasn't living the life I had planned to be living by then. Comparing what I wanted to be doing with my actual reality caused me a lot of stress for months, and this was stress I didn't even become aware of until halfway through 2021. Stress had become so commonplace that I couldn't even see it – it had become my default feeling. I saw myself as a victim of circumstance rather than accepting what was a global catastrophe. There were many worse situations to be in, and this is something I knew, but it was still difficult not to feel like I was stuck. Rather than getting my own way, I felt trapped (in my head) in Cork working a job I didn't like. I'd been kept there as a result of a worldwide shutdown. I was catastrophising everything because I felt hard-done by. Nothing, in reality, was as bad as it seemed to me. The toys were being thrown from the pram. I couldn't let myself accept reality and make the most of it, so instead my mental health took a battering.

I became resentful of my job, and my life in general. A bitterness developed inside me and my once optimistic and positive mindset twisted into a horrible cynicism. I saw people I knew on social media living 'better' lives elsewhere in more fulfilling places and this drove me insane. What I failed to understand is that I could also live this 'better' life right where I was, if I learned to appreciate what I already had instead of longing for things I couldn't have right then and there. If I stopped being childish and demanding, I could find happiness in whatever situation I found myself in.

During that first lockdown, between March of 2020 and the end of the summer, I was writing more than ever, working out more than ever, putting more time and energy into my blog and website. I was productive but for all the wrong reasons. It wasn't coming from a place of passion, it was coming from a place of insecurity. I wasn't leading any sort of life I considered to be fulfilling, so I felt that by plunging into different endeavours, I could at least make a dent in the road ahead. I could at least make something of myself in a place I didn't want to be. This mindset caused me to stop taking pleasure in the work. I no longer enjoyed the process – I just wanted to rush to the end. I wanted instant gratification, and so every moment I wasn't 'achieving' was a moment of stress, which meant that most of time I existed with a clenched jaw and a sore back. I was stressed for so long that I could no longer even see the stress. I had become the stress.

By the time summer ended, although I wasn't in a bad place, it didn't feel like I was in any place at all. I was sort of floating. The numbness of depression had slowly taken over again in its quiet way. I had been so caught up with looking at what everyone else was doing that I hadn't even felt it come along. I wasn't enjoying anything. Nothing was fulfilling, and everything I gave time to was an effort to keep busy, to prevent my mind from becoming idle, because when the quiet settled in, negative thoughts about myself and how I was living blasted in my mind at full volume. It felt like I was watching myself live half a life instead of actively participating in a full one. I was on the outside looking in at life whilst everyone else got on with theirs. And this is an awful, awful place to be in.

As the summer drew in, I was seeing someone who probably lived too far away and was probably too different to me for it to work out in the long run.

Even reading that back sounds like bullshit. Of course, long distance can be tricky but we lived near enough that you could travel to the other person with a couple of hours if you wanted to. The real reason it wasn't going to work out was because I was looking for excuses, such as distance or a difference in personality, to end things. Things were going fine and I began to feel trapped, so I started looking for problems. That's the real issue, and it's always been the real issue. If I could have been more emotionally advanced, or even just better at communicating how I was feeling, then I would have known this girl was great, and that it could have worked out if I wanted it to. There wasn't anything wrong with the way I was feeling

– these fears are totally natural – but there was an issue with not talking about how I was feeling. I have often done this in the past. Instead of telling my partner how I feel, I hide it away and end things abruptly. I think I've always been reluctant to talk about how I'm feeling because I think I'm wrong to be feeling that way. I'm wrong to be unsure, or scared or reluctant. And because I attach guilt to feeling these things, I hide my emotions from people, because of the shame of feeling them.

Anyway, this girl was great craic, and we enjoyed each other's company. She didn't like certain aspects of how I spent my time, how I spent too much time on Twitter for example, or that I wasn't as outgoing as she was. She was incredibly social and bubbly, whereas I'm generally only very social with people I'm comfortable around. We argued over those kinds of things when she wanted me to be different, I think.

We weren't exclusive, and because of the distance, I had only seen her three times by the end of September. When the distance restrictions kicked back in – one could only travel within their own county - it meant we couldn't legally see each other and things sort of fizzled away. The lockdown did the heavy lifting of the break-up for us. There was no big conversation needed because we both knew what lockdown meant. I felt a certain sense of relief, but this relief was based on a maladaptive issue. I was relieved because my desire to run from a relationship had been satiated. Relief always feels good, but it may not always be as a result of something that is good for you. Relief can come when you successfully avoid going to the doctor when you need to, for example. It's not always a certainty that it's the best move. The way things panned out, if we played by all the rules I wouldn't have been able to see her again legally until sometime in mid-2021, a good 8 months later (it would have been May 2021, to be exact).

A few short weeks later, I had to isolate because I was a close contact for Covid. I texted her then, mainly because we weren't totally done with, and also because I felt alone, but she just brushed me off. She didn't care that I felt alone, probably because she also felt alone. Neither of us were really there for the other, despite having said we would be at one stage. This might be a factor in mental health that goes under the radar sometimes which is worth addressing here. We all say we're there to talk to if anyone is feeling a certain way. We say we're always there for others. These sentiments are common place online and well-intended, but they're often empty gestures. When it comes down to the practicality of being there, how many of us actually are? I'd argue very few, and I don't mean that from a place of judgement, just as an observation.

I'd argue we're all so caught up in our own lives that promoting positive vibes about 'always being there' only works to make us feel better ourselves. In reality, if someone told us they weren't feeling so good, we might not know what to say, and therefore say nothing. This is often due to a lack of knowledge or for fear of saying the wrong thing, which is a fair concern. However, most people just want to be heard rather than wanting you to give them the answers. When we're reaching out because of loneliness, the last thing we need is no response at all.

On top of this, we might not even realise we should check in with people to begin with. Mental health has become such a trend in today's world that we of course say that we care about other's mental health, but when it comes down to it, I find it strange that we leave it up to the people who are struggling to reach out. We put the onus on the sufferer to open up voluntarily – which is extremely difficult to do if you're going through it – and this allows the rest of us to alleviate responsibility. Not only do we get away with not checking in with the people around us, but we can feel good about ourselves, knowing that we tweeted empty promises of 'always being here to talk.'

It's quite human to not want to admit to any of that. None of us ever want to admit when we might be falling short. None of us want to openly admit that we are in fact, not always here to chat, or that we don't care as much as we say we do. We don't want to believe we can be callous or self-serving or cruel, but we all have the potential to be. We all let people down, or we put our own needs first. It's only natural. We all have this potential for falseness. We're not born good or bad. We're born, and we do what we think is right and sometimes what we think is the right thing isn't the right thing at all. We preserve ourselves first and this can lead to letting other people down.

We must endeavour to remember that the villain often thinks they're the good guy. So when we fall short, or even consider that we could fall short, I think it makes us uncomfortable because it suggests we aren't as good as we want to believe. That's why we always say we'll be there for people when they need us, because the opposite doesn't sound good. However, the opposite is far more common. It's far more common for us to reach out and get nothing back, especially in the age of the online ego. It's far more common for us to struggle and for people to do nothing because they're too caught up in their own lives.

All of the anxiety that came with my close contact with Covid turned out to be for nothing in the end, which is a fairly good summation of anxiety in and of itself. It's a great deal of suffering for no good reason. One of the many things my father taught me as a young fella who was obsessed with the world's imminent demise was, '*Don't worry about things you cannot control,*' yet that's exactly what I had just been doing for consecutive days. I had no control over whether I got the virus or not, or if I had passed it on or not, but I still drove myself demented from worrying over it.

I escaped coronavirus on that occasion. The same thing happened the second time around too, early in 2021. Regardless of my lack of positive testing, I still had to do a 14-day isolation, which was quite a lonely time. Being alone with your thoughts, without any human interaction aside from the pseudo interactions found online can be a challenge on any day, let alone during a time when it was suggested that you may well kill someone if you leave the house, or even the bedroom. Here I was then, facing down some time spent alone which was forced upon me by circumstance.

Now, it may come as a shock to you that I'm a bit of a loner by nature. I think I inherited that characteristic from my father, who has always been comically outspoken about how he is happy to spend all of his time alone. Tongue-in-cheek of course, but there's a certain truth to it. We're quite alike temperamentally. My father has taught me many invaluable things by living; the difference between what is right and what is easy, and the value of being able to spend time alone are two of the more important ones. It's not that we don't like other people, it's that we're quite happy to spend long periods of time alone when it suits. I enjoy being around others, in fact. But I'm also just as happy on my own, most of the time.

My own company isn't something I've feared in the past. So in that regard, isolation didn't change much for me in terms of scheduling. I postponed a few coffees with friends and skipped a visit home that week. Other than that, I generally spent my spare time in those days doing extra writing and running which are generally solo endeavours. It was more or less business as usual. However, there was no element of freedom, which made me feel trapped. I couldn't meet people even if I wanted to, and this often leads to feeling lonely. I won't feel lonely if I choose to spend time alone. So long as I could have chosen differently everything is fine. The choice appears to be fundamental to how the alone time makes us feel.

I wouldn't say there's a desire for me to be alone.

Desire isn't the correct word for it. Inclination might be better suited. If you did an experiment, I'd probably choose alone time over social time more often than not. There's always something to think about, or read, or write down, or watch. Complaining of boredom in this age just seems lazy. In days gone by I wouldn't find myself in any particular anguish from being in between days of living on my own. But it's not always perfect or easy, and this has little to do with boredom. I can drum up a wicked afternoon of anxiety if I don't stay disciplined in my thinking. If I begin to compare myself, to say, other writers online who I consider more successful than me, I become entirely engrossed in an anxious spiral. I compare myself to people, and note my failures in comparison to their brilliance and I hate myself for it on sunny afternoons. That particular year - when there was even more time spent alone – meant spending more time online than you normally would, and this in turn led to more comparison. It takes a level of discipline I didn't yet possess to stop comparing myself to other people I've never even met.

Mid-October was upon us once my isolation ended. The weather had changed and there was a bite in the air. Most mornings my windows were edged by condensation and my feet were cold under the desk while I worked. Gentle ice seduced the grass outside and cars began to need extra time to defrost in the early hours. For some reason, the idea of facing a second lockdown single was much more dread-inducing than it had been during the summer. I didn't mind at all the first time around, but now, since I had gone through a number of failed romances in the months previous, I not only felt alone, but also felt as though I was incapable of making something last. This all came whilst on the brink of not being able to see anyone for months. I had a sense of what it felt like to be alone in full lockdown, and this wasn't something I wanted to jump back into. Juxtaposed against this was the realisation that I was more self-destructive in relationships than I cared to admit. I felt lonelier than ever, even though I was alone by my own hand one again.

I remember spending strings of entire weekends alone during October and November. Not being able to meet up with friends, the fellas I lived with rightfully spending time with girlfriends they cared for, I found myself alone at night, distracting myself with Netflix and feeling very sorry. I was anxious, and oftentimes I was in a low mood, but I was fine outwardly. When phone calls with my parents came around, I told them everything was fine because I didn't want them to worry. Rather than open up about how lonely I felt, I made sure that I matched their energy. Old habits of faking emotions came back and I reflected a version of me who was coping perfectly to the world.

Looking back now, I was definitely casting myself as a victim who was being hard-done by. What I failed to grasp however, was that I was also the one who had victimised myself. When I did feel low during lockdown, I also felt guilty because, overall, I did in fact have it quite good, relatively speaking. I wasn't out of work, or out of pocket, and it wasn't like I had no friends or family. Feeling low despite all of this only made me feel worse, because there was an added element of being too self-absorbed and lacking in gratitude.

When you're self-destructive, you'll constantly find yourself looking for excuses to explain this behaviour, but not matter what, you eventually face up to the truth that you have only yourself to blame. When this happens you can either accept who you are – faults and all – and begin to do the work required to grow, or you can ignore the problem and hope it magically goes away. I was alone because I was difficult. I was alone because my expectations for love were unrealistic and unachievable. This was the reality I ignored for so long. In many ways, I felt broken just then before we went into a second lockdown, and I worried over what would become of me in the winter of 2020. It can be jarring to feel like you've finally gotten to a good place only to fall from the pedestal you've built yourself. I only thought I had healed, but I hadn't actually addressed any of my ongoing issues. Instead I used the distraction of a busy life to keep me afloat, never having enough time to act destructively because I was only on the way to the next thing – be it work, or training, or a writing session. Then, when the pandemic came, along with lockdowns and isolations, I had nowhere to hide. There was no longer so much going on that I could avoid my issues. I had all the time in the world, and my relationships problems in particular revealed themselves. For most of my life I had blamed everyone else for things going wrong, but in lockdown I found out that I was the problem more often than not.

And while this was going on, my social media feeds would lead you to believe I was thriving. I certainly didn't feel like I was. I felt lost. I thought having a new book coming out would help me to find my way again. It scared me how little it mattered, how little I cared about that second boo. It scared the fuck out of me to be honest. Writing was my crutch since college and all of sudden, not even that was helping.

Now here's a modern problem which we don't know the long-term effects of. How we project versions of ourselves online which are rarely anything like how we really are. How is it that a person such as myself can be struggling with profound loneliness and sadness, yet appear to be 'living the life' in the online world? Why don't we express how we really feel online? Why do we feel like we can't tell the truth? How come I can't say I feel lonely online and not feel very strange about it?

These are questions with complex answers. Social media can be a good tool, but oftentimes it does more harm than anything else. Quite often, we fall into the trap of comparing our lives to the highlight reels of others, and we turn to social media to validate our intrinsic value, rather than understanding our worth internally. We have the ability to create who we want to be online, which means we can easily lie to the world about who and how we are. We can be sat in our rooms overwhelmed by sadness and project successful, upbeat versions ourselves into the world without anyone even noticing. Why is that okay to do? Why have we created spaces where only positive emotions are allowed? We're beings that experience both negative and positive feelings, so why do we act like we shouldn't feel some of them?

I suppose it's an unwritten social contract in ways. It's fine to say you're doing well. Positive sentiments are encouraged. Sure don't we all love that? And if we don't love when a person is doing well, we at least love to talk shite about them posting about how good their lives are. People love to hope for other people to fail, for them to fall from grace. *Schadenfreude* is as rampant as anything in this age of attention-addiction. So whether people want to see you thrive or fail, everyone gets something from you flexing your pseudo-positive achievements online.

However, if you post some real, honest, heartfelt emotions, feelings that may not be positive, well, then things can get uncomfortable. It's almost as if we're expected to suppress our emotions to keep everyone else comfortable. You can become distanced from your peers if you post about your sadness rather than say, post pictures of you at the beach. People only want you to be funny, or hold certain opinions, or to look a certain way. Anything outside of that is considered taboo. And this is maybe why we all have these artificial versions of ourselves online. But it also highlights the problem. Projecting false versions of ourselves explains how a person like me, or a person struggling even more so, like Erbie did before he died, might appear to everyone else around them to be doing perfectly fine, when they're actually losing a battle no one knows about. People are constantly posting made-up variants of themselves and hiding behind them because those are the values we, as a society have determined to be important.

We prefer fake happiness to genuine emotions of any kind.

That's an awfully scary precedent to set. We've created an illusion of 'the good life' so strong that you can't even see the red flags of mental struggle around you, because so many people have been conditioned not to show them online whatsoever. It's impossible to see real human connection is a world that filters out most of our emotional catalogue. The online world only wants a certain version of you, and that version of you is not allowed to be imperfect, and is certainly not allowed to feel sad. At a certain point it becomes impossible for many people to speak up about how they're feeling at all, because the online world has made them believe that feeling unhappy or not living the 'best life' (whatever the fuck that means) has some sort of negative connotation about who they are attached to it. People feel bad about themselves for not leading lives that make other people jealous. They feel bad about the life they lead because it doesn't resemble the ones they see every day on social media. We see people who are constantly happy in far off paradises and it makes us feel bad about ourselves, because our lives don't look the same way. And this snowballs into feeling sad or lonely, which we then feel bad about because the people we see online are so happy. So instead, we pretend we're not sad, or that we're not lonely. We fake happiness in the hope that if we fake it long enough it will become true without addressing any of the issues. And this just leads to bigger issues further down the road when everything comes to a head.

The Lesson

That first two week isolation I had to do in 2020 allowed me some time to reflect. When you feel lonely, it makes you insecure and this, in turn, makes you read rejection in places it may not be coming from. I was upset because I didn't get a reply from a girl with whom things were going badly with, and I took this as a personal slight against me rather than a response that was reasonable given the situation.

When our sense of self-confidence is compromised we'll look for confirmations of this in the behaviours of others. So when I felt lonely during those two weeks, I began to seek confirmations of this. I thought people didn't like me or didn't want to talk to me. There was no proof of any of it, but when you're in this mind state and spending too much time online, seeing other people lead perfect lives, it's easy to find yourself some evidence.

That part of 2020 was extremely challenging, but I learned some key things during it, so we will consider those tough days worthwhile. The takeaways here are two-fold. Firstly, worrying about things we cannot control, such as whether or not we have a potentially deadly virus, or about the opinions and behaviours of other people, makes little to no sense, and so we should prevent ourselves from doing this as often as possible. Anxiety, when it is being misused, is nothing more than time wasted on imaginary things.

Secondly, we learned that social media, when used irresponsibly, can cause you to juxtapose your external self with your real, internal self. You will not only compare yourself to others, but you will also compare who you are now with the imaginary version of you that you want to be. Social media can disrupt mental health, and so we're better served using it as a tool rather than as a distraction.

Don't worry about things you can't control, and don't compare your life to the ones you see online.

The Grip of Jealousy

When life isn't moving in the direction you want it to, or it doesn't resemble the life you might prefer to have, it's very easy to look outside yourself and find that other people are leading better lives than you, and then resenting them for it. In 2020, and in the beginnings of 2021, I felt lost. I'd never really felt truly lost before. I'd certainly felt stuck, like I knew where I was going but couldn't find a way to get there. At least when you're stuck you can fall back on a routine, trust the process, and wait it out. You can rest assured because you still know where you want to go. It's not so simple when you're lost because you don't have something to aim at. You don't know where it is you're going which means you don't have any idea of how to come out of the fog.

Being lost means you're both stuck and unsure of where it is you want to be heading. Towards the end of 2020, I was still writing but it didn't feel like it was amounting to much of anything. The rejections were piling up for a novel I'd written which I didn't care too much about (which explains why it wasn't getting anywhere). I was working in a job which brought no sense of fulfilment. I was living in a way that didn't inspire me. There was nothing that excited me to the point of passion. I was still in a cycle of loneliness due to production anxiety. I was bad at expressing my emotions. I was languishing in a big way – I was going through the motions of my life without any real attachment or meaning. There was no point in the future that I was aiming at and there was nothing in my life that made me feel grounded. The structure of a routine no longer existed, now that 70% of my life was spent in the room I slept in. The panic of being lost had set in, like when you were 9 years old and you couldn't find your mother in the supermarket, and you began to think that you'd never be found. Often when we are lost or fed up, we compare what we have going on to the lives of others, and in this circumstance, when life is less than ideal, the comparisons lead to envy more so than a feeling of reassurance.

During bouts of perceived underperformance, jealousy can be more toxic than anything.

Jealousy is a natural state of mind – it allows you to identify that which you want the most – but it can be detrimental if you allow it to fester. A sprinkling of jealousy from time to time is actually useful, as you can use it to fuel yourself and take inspiration from. You can use jealousy to identify what you want, compare that place to where you are, and plot a route to make up the distance. However, when you're not sure of where you're going, and the envy serves only to reconfirm that you're lost and possibly failing, a jealous mind can cause distress in any manner of ways, and this inevitably leads to bitterness, which causes us to be miserable in our lives.

Jealousy also suggests that a person needs external validation to be happy. I know that during this time in my life, I was insecure about my writing ability, and so I was jealous of the attention given to other writers. My sense of value was externalised, which meant I wouldn't be content until I received proof from outside myself that I was succeeding. And so, I was jealous of other people, not necessarily because I wanted their lives, but because I wanted the attention they received for the work they were doing. I remember noticing it in myself first online – the great comparison tool of our time. Writers who were both strangers and people I knew were getting book deals, winning awards, receiving high praise from big names – all deserved undoubtedly – but it used to drive me mental because of how insecure I felt.

All day on Twitter I'd see how everyone else was winning, yet there I was, idling away with rejections letters hitting my inbox every other day. It was disheartening as I interpreted their wins as direct losses for me. My lack of progress juxtaposed with the success of others had made my mind a toxic vat that churned away night and day. Framing it this way caused my self-confidence to plummet, and so my mind began to look for more confirmations of this failure. Bias had set in, and instead of seeing reality objectively, I was skewing it to fit the hypothesis that I was failing because that's what I believed (confirmation bias at its finest).

I began taking everything personally. I was connecting dots where no dots existed. Rejection letters were an attack on me, and in my mind the agents and publishers who sent them had some personal vendetta. People didn't want me to succeed, and suddenly everyone was against me. If I had let myself release these emotions it would have manifested briefly as anger or frustration, but I constantly pretended that I wasn't jealous because I was ashamed of myself, and so I bottled up the emotions inside. My thoughts became toxic and I started viewing every interaction I had via the internet and beyond with a cynical, pessimistic eye. There was no good to be found, and everything anyone did was self-serving and disingenuous to my mind. This was my war against the world for failing to fulfil my desires. I deserved what I wanted and I hadn't gotten my way, and this was a fault of theirs and not of mine.

Oh, what a silly way to think that is – I hadn't gotten my way at exactly the moment I wanted it, so I blamed everyone else for this. How common is this mindset?

We rarely want to take responsibility for our shortcomings. None of us wants to know the role we play in our own demise because it makes us uncomfortable. It's uncomfortable to look plainly at ourselves and see the villainous, and lazy, and childish parts. We all have these parts but none of us enjoy looking upon them. They highlight the reality of out imperfection, so it becomes easier to externalise their existence. Rather than our failures being a result of our lack of work ethic or commitment or ability, it becomes the fault of the conspirators who work against us. We blame bosses with grudges, other people who are jealous of us, timing, and a lack of fairness, for our inability to succeed in the present. The phrase '*What is for me won't pass me*' has become a common mechanism to deal with these feelings of inadequacy.

Instead of facing up to the fact that we may not be good enough for what we want right now, and trying to improve, we take comfort in the fact that somehow we played no role in the outcome. We force ourselves to believe that the big, bad universe willed us away from our goal, because this makes us feel better about ourselves. We don't have to face our inadequacy or our incompetence if we believe that things happened the way they did for a reason. We don't have to admit that we didn't do enough work if we put the blame on someone, or something else. It's not uncommon for this mindset to be the default. I can understand why it's desirable too – it stops us from feeling negatively about ourselves, regardless of whether the negative things are true.

Social media being intertwined with everyone's life propagates this sense of entitlement, this sense of instant gratification, and so when we don't get our own way, the culture of narcissism tells us it's okay to throw a tantrum for not getting it. We are told that we have been hard-done by rather than being told that we failed due to our own shortcomings. Personal responsibility is thrown out the window

As has become a common thread throughout these reflections, awareness of a maladaptive behaviour isn't enough to disrupt it. It became clear to me after some time of feeling jealous of others that the world wasn't against me, and nothing was personal, because nobody knew me. And this was probably the crux of the matter if I could have been honest with myself – nobody knew me and I wanted to be known. The reason the jealousy was manifesting was because others were in places in their careers where they were being seen, and I was invisible. I was craving validation, and notoriety, and this is something I'd have denied until the cows came home. But it was true, I know that now. So when I saw others who had what I wanted, it caused me to lose confidence and my sense of value. Comparing myself to them hurt my ego and that's where all the envy stemmed from. I'd see people living their lives, doing nothing at all to harm me, and I would become stressed and jealous and awful.

I was a bitter little man for months. I spent too much time online instead of putting that time to use, and it only worked to further coagulate my bitterness. Not only was I not where I wanted to be, but I wasn't doing the work required to get there either. The jealousy was compounded by a lack of progress on my part, and this became cyclical. I suppose it made sense in ways. It was only inevitable that it would happen. Considering how isolated I was in those months and years, and how cynical I had become. I spent hours upon hours alone, toiling away and seeing all these other people doing so well when I was not. Instead of living my life, trusting the work, and understanding that these things take a lot of time and patience, I was distressing, because things weren't happening for me immediately. The trend of instant gratification had absorbed me, and because I wanted my success to happen now, I acted like I was entitled to it now, too. So, every moment these successes weren't happening was a moment of frustration on some level. It was a recipe for disaster.

Bitterness is like anxiety's angry cousin. It works in a similar way. It makes you think and believe things which there is no evidence for, just like anxiety does. Where they differ is the direction of blame. Whereas anxiety points inward and over-blames the self, bitterness points outwards and blames everyone else.

This makes bitterness more destructive, I think.

When you're bitter you don't just hate yourself, you hate the people who make you feel bad about yourself, too. You blame other people for the fact that you are falling short, at least from your own misinformed perspective. You begin to distance yourself from anyone who makes you feel this way and you assign a negative sentiment to who they are. You'll know you feel bitter when you dislike someone for no other reason than that they are doing well and their success makes you feel inferior. When a person does nothing to do you, but you still feel bad about yourself because of them, then this is *your* problem. But we very rarely accept this as our problem because then we have to take responsibility rather than continuing to assign blame.

Other people shouldn't have to dampen their shine to make us feel better. Bitterness is that shite talk you take part in when there's a person doing well for themselves, and you want to make yourself feel better by saying strings of negative sentiments about them. We've all been bitter at some stage, and that's fine. Just like it's fine and appropriate to be sad sometimes, it's fine to be bitter in certain moments. The problem emerges when you stay in a state of bitterness for long periods. That's been the issue with all of the mental health problems I've had – it's not that the way I was feeling was wrong, rather it was the fact that I was feeling this way for weeks and months on end which then became problematic.

What I came to realise over time, and what we all need to be aware of, is that it is not the other person's fault, nor their responsibility, to manage how we feel. Another person shouldn't have to take responsibility for how their success and good fortune makes other people feel about themselves. Insecurities breed bitterness, and we need to at least be aware of why we feel negatively towards people who have never done anything to us. The key to overcoming bitterness and the stress that comes with it, is to look inward and identify what insecurity exists within us which are making us feel this way. We become bitter because we feel bad about ourselves, and we feel bad about ourselves because of where we place our value.

If you place value on being known, like I did, then you will never be known well enough. You will never have enough followers and the press you get will never be enough press. You will constantly be miserable as you chase down this invisible dragon. Similarly, if you value physical attractiveness you might find yourself being bitter towards people who are 'successful' in this domain, or if you value money you will become bitter towards people who have more of it than you do, and so on. Bitterness is a defence mechanism to protect us from the truth, and the truth is that we feel inadequate in the world. Bitterness allows us to lash out at other people rather than accept out limitations. It's much easier to blame the people around us than it is to take responsibility for ourselves. Being angry at others is less mentally taxing than the hatred we could potentially show ourselves, and so bitterness is the destructive mechanism by which we protect ourselves from intense self-hate. *"It's not my fault, it's their fault."*

This has become a normalised trend in our world. It's led to much division and hate and almost feels irreparable. What exactly can you do when you're being motivated by jealousy? When you find yourself angry or stressed or anxious as a result of someone else's achievements, how do you work around that? It's not an easy position to be in, and it's quite difficult to be honest enough with yourself to admit that the reason you dislike someone at all is because you envy what they have. Our egos are reluctant for us to know that truth. We'll often rationalize it by saying that these people are 'bad' people who have everything good happen to them, but again, this just makes it easier for us to consolidate. We use cognitive dissonance repeatedly to avoid addressing the root of our issues. We can justify our anger and frustrations if we think they are reasonable reactions. But when it comes to bitterness and jealousy, we're usually acting poorly because of this reluctance to accept our own flaws.

This envy and bitterness extended beyond the realm of writing, too. It got to a point where people who had different opinions to my own about movies I liked began to make me angry, and it was then that I knew there was a serious problem emerging. I know it might seem dramatic to say that based on such trivial things, but that's sort of the point. Trivial things which never made me envious or angry in the past were now infuriating me. There was something going on. The envy had morphed into full-fledged resentment for a lot of things, and the more time I spent online the worse it seemed to get.

Yet, I couldn't pull myself away from Twitter in particular because I was flat out addicted to the serotonin it gave me.

I was jealous of people for two reasons. I was jealous of anyone who was doing well in the field I wanted to do well in. There's nothing wrong with healthy levels of jealousy to keep ourselves motivated, but I harboured too much and that became an issue. The second reason is social media addiction. I was addicted to Twitter for months on end, and so I was jealous and bitter towards anyone who was deemed popular on the platform. It took me an age to admit that to myself because it felt like an embarrassing thing to be true. I had an addiction to the idea of being known and that was making my brain toxic for myself, and for the people around me. When I became aware of this, I began to take note of any time something made me angry and then I'd ask myself why that thing in particular annoyed me. It was a make-shift form of Cognitive Behavioural Therapy which I used to figure out why I was getting stressed and angry when I spent time online. Far too often, the annoyance I felt was rooted in jealousy, rather than any rational reason for being angry (e.g. being attacked, insulted, ridiculed etc.).

I believed that every time someone else won, I was losing, and so for a time I couldn't be happy for anyone. Additionally, when other people won it felt like more of an accomplishment than when I won. I brushed my successes aside because I was fixated on other people. So not only was I resentful of others, I wasn't even giving myself recognition for the work I had done. If you think like this for long enough, it's easy to see how your mind will become a totally destructive place to exist.

Once I wised up to my jealousy, and began to clock it every time I got annoyed or stressed, it slowly became less of an issue. After some time and a lot of patience I was able to be genuinely happy for other people doing well. Rather than be jealous of people achieving, I learned to accept that their journeys didn't, and couldn't, impact my own progression, which removed the barriers to being happy for their earned achievements. Instead, I used the jealousy I harboured as motivation to work harder and aspire to be in their position one day.

Now people who achieved inspired me to work, instead of causing me stress and anxiety. Rather than wishing that they'd fail, I worked so that I could win, too. It's not easy to look at yourself and see the green monster of envy engraved. It doesn't make you look good, nor does it make you feel good. But it is better to reflect and accept an honest image than it is to pretend the image is perfect.

You can begin to work on a cracked mirror, but you can't if you won't admit that the mirror is broken in the first place.

The Lesson

The lesson here is in understanding how easy it can be to fall into bitterness. Bitterness will convince us that the world and the people in it are awful, and that everyone is working against us. If we view the world through this lens then the world does become a hellish fire, where we can only see people for their worst. It makes us distrustful, resentful and cynical. When you think everyone is out to get you, then you assume the worst of intentions. It's dehumanising and painful. It's entitled to think that we deserve things immediately just because we want them. You ignore the fact that others have worked for years, if not decades, for the thing you want right now. That's what I was doing then. I wanted to be successful and when it wasn't happening instantly, everyone who was successful morphed into a personal attack on me.

How we view the world, and other people, affects our reality. If we choose to see the worst in people, then the world will seem like a worse place than it could be if you looked at it differently. I was lucky that I was able to become aware enough to see it happening eventually. I can only imagine how I would have turned out if I continued to let jealousy run the show. It's often an undetectable sickness, until one day you wake up and realise how the green monster has ruined your life, and indeed your character. The worry is that there are so many people wrapped up by their bitterness that they can't see it for what it is. And so, they continue to believe the true version of the world that exists is the one that's on fire. But this isn't true if you can get your head out of the flames.

Existing in this world as a lonely and bitter person is not conducive with good mental wellbeing. Every step towards the fire makes it more difficult to come back from. In a world that appears to be dominated by anger and resentment and bitterness, the most rebellious thing we can do is be relentlessly sound. The fight against this sort of corruption begins with genuinely enjoying who you are, trusting that things will work out in some way, and making as many people as we can feel good along the way. You can want to achieve your goals and still be happy for other people who are further along the road. These aren't mutually exclusive. This may be difficult to see now, but it's true. There is plenty of space for both. And it's much easier on your own mental health to be sound, than it is to be resentful.

The takeaway here: Jealousy will dim your light if you let it. Identify what exactly is causing you to become envious, and cut it out. Stop being bitter, and be sound.

The Slow Death of Mental Fortitude

In 1517, a dance plague struck the city of Strasbourg, affecting over 400, and killing tens of people. This isn't some sort of metaphor; the people affected literally couldn't stop dancing. Documentation of this event in history is poor and so it is unclear how or why this plague broke out in the city. I've always assumed that a raw form of MDMA was discovered and became rampant in a sub-population of the community, causing them to want to dance for hours on end, but this is merely amusing speculation. After some days the dancing stopped and many participants passed away from exhaustion and dehydration. This was a very strange event caused mainly by conformity.

I have wondered about his many times over the last two years. No doubt this curiosity was brought on by the monotony of being in between waves of a global pandemic. When there's not much you can do outside of the house, I always find myself going down the rabbit hole for stories like this one. Aside from the somewhat humorous nature of the tale, I wondered about the aspect of the human psyche that causes us to conform without question. Surely not everyone, if anyone, was off their heads on MDMA during the dance plague. It would make sense but there's no evidence to suggest they were. Realistically, most people just saw others dancing and joined in for the craic, and they all kept dancing so long as everyone else kept dancing. A dancing fever, if you will.

The summer of 2020 saw a fever-pitch of conformity and maybe that's why I was thinking so much about this dance plague. I don't know whether it was all bad, but it was definitely noticeably at a new height. You could probably put that down to lockdown and people being driven demented by flawed thought patterns. I not-so-quietly watched from the outer reaches of social media circles, as people conformed, pandered, virtue-signalled, postured, condescended, and all the rest to attain some sort of clout to feel some sort of meaning in their own lives. This is the nature of social media, though, where people say the 'right' things in exchange for cheap serotonin.

I was quickly realising the danger of social media, on the back of realising I was addicted to it. Instead of trying to find purpose in real life, many of us chase the validation of strangers in a fake world. There's a poetic strain to it that makes one melancholic on a Sunday morning. And this is by no means implying that I'm any different. I've regularly fallen victim to the trappings of cheap serotonin.

It worried me far more as the months went on, how easy it is to set people against each other. All you really need to do is set up a dichotomy, and to do this all you need is a point of contention which evokes visceral emotion and a lot of strong opinions. Some will claim to be in the middle of both sides, but will swing marginally towards one of the poles eventually. Once you find yourself within a camp you become polarised and learn to broach anyone from the other camp with anger and distrust. There is no such thing as a nuanced opinion online, at least not in the loudest conversations, and as soon as someone has a differing opinion they become your enemy. Once this is going on, people stop caring about objective truth online, they only care about being right – they only care about their own truth. When you only care about being right you become terribly easy to control and manipulate because in this world what is 'right' can be distorted.

Suddenly people no longer care about what's objectively right for everyone, they only care about what is right for their own tribe. Imagine a world where every conversation is a battleground, and the truth doesn't matter so long as you win. How we feel is suddenly more important than the truth of a given situation, which means nobody has to admit to getting anything wrong. That's what discourse online has become in many ways.

When you're not satisfied with how your life is going, the world appears to be weighed against you, even though you're the one with the knife to your own neck. I wrote about this in an earlier essay with regard to jealousy – we prefer to attack others instead of accepting our own flawed selves. We tend not to want to face up to our own shortcomings so we externalise any reasons for why we're not succeeding the way we think we ought to be.

It was around then that I knew we were kind of doomed to dance around our words for the rest of time. People are becoming more and more certain that the things they believe are true, and there is no apparent room for differences. Doubting oneself is uncomfortable, yes, but living in certainty is truly ridiculous, and has the potential to become dangerous. Voltaire said that hundreds of years ago, but it's a message seemingly ignored in today's world. People are so certain of the moral superiority of their opinions now, and this leaves no room for progress. Instead it breeds conflict.

I've seen this new trend of trance-like conformity to whatever the accepted narrative is compared to religion, and in fairness it seems accurate. If you don't agree with the narrative you are a heathen and therefore wrong or bad. You are outside the belief system, which means you are a problem. Thinking independently, outside of the prescribed idealogue is considered controversial. There is no room for any individual thought, you are either a part of the hive-mind or you are part of the problem. There is no room for you to agree to an extent but have a variation of the mainstream opinion. Certain beliefs are God and if you don't believe every single facet of the Good Word then you aren't serving your new God.

If you're reading this and think it's concerning, please know that there's a good chance you've been part of the hive-mind at some point. If you've ever posted online about some cause, not because you've researched it and genuinely care, but because it was trending and everyone else was posting, and you felt like you had to, this is that conformity in motion. Whenever you do something because you feel some sort of social pressure to be seen participating, this is the mechanism in work.

There was a point during the Black Lives Matter movement of 2020 where everyone posted a black square on their Instagram pages in solidarity. This wasn't done because everyone had conducted in-depth research. Oh God no. People just saw other people posting a black square and thought that it was a good idea to do, so that they could look like good people in the eyes of their anonymous peers. It did nothing for the cause, but people were able to give themselves a nice pat on the back and feel like they did something genuinely good. Without doing anything of actual impact, people begin to feel morally superior to say, people who decided posting a black square on their Instagram page did nothing for anyone.

I say this as one of the people who, historically, has often conformed out of fear of being ostracised, and out of some sense that my participation is mandatory. This isn't a preaching-from-the-mound situation. It's a cautionary tale suggesting that conformity due to social coercion makes nobody a good person. Yet it makes people feel morally superior. Which results in conflict, which results in division, which results in an easily controllable world.

So, 2020 saw the doctrines of ideology take over the internet. That distinction is important. You'd often be on Twitter and find yourself up to your neck in utter madness, but it's important to remember most people aren't on Twitter, and so the platform isn't representative of the majority. You'll read some shite on there that will suggest the world has recently been unhinged from a door that no longer exists. In ways it has, but the insanity of this form of religious movement isn't as widespread as you might imagine. However, if you spend a lot of time online, which all-too-many of us did during the pandemic, it's easy to get caught up in the ways people think. There are many, many radical and loud personas online who automatically assume the worst intentions of nearly everyone else, and it's important to be able to take a break from this.

The woman I had been seeing during September of 2020 mentioned that she thought it was strange that I used Twitter so much. She said she didn't get my attraction to that platform, and thought it was weird. It was a clear sign of disdain for her that I was so caught up in it. I took offence to her saying this at the time, and told her how I felt judged. And, I did feel judged, as if I was doing something wrong for using the app. Looking back now, I know I felt offended mainly because her words had struck a nerve, but I hadn't yet come around to admitting I was addicted. She could see the pitfalls of using it long before I did. I felt judged, not because she was out of pocket, but because I knew she was right and I didn't like it.

The only reason I took offence was because somewhere in my head she had clocked something which was true. I think we only ever get truly annoyed at people's words if we know what they're saying is accurate. They've addressed a flaw we've been trying our best to avoid looking at, and this makes us feel insecure and vulnerable, so we become angered. If someone insults us using points which are clearly untrue, we don't usually have as strong an emotional reaction. We're able to brush it off easily enough because they are not flaws we have hidden away in the dark.

It's only when someone addresses something we dislike about ourselves, something that is true and ugly and shameful, that we become upset. We don't like it when others force us to look upon ourselves. So I took offence to her comment because I was addicted to Twitter, and I simply would not admit it to myself. Instead of addressing an issue within me, I blamed her for making me upset. Externalising the blame once again, instead of internalising the responsibility.

During 2020, Twitter was an absolute garbage fire of hatred and outrage. You'd come away from the platform having lost several thousand braincells, guaranteed. Between, lockdown, and US racial tensions, and no one having anything to do, it seemed like the world was more angry and divided than it had ever been, and it became an addictive discourse to observe and engage with. But this came at a cost. You can't engage in such divisive and anxiety-inducing discourse and come away unharmed. During this time my anxiety levels were through the roof and I never linked it to how much time I was spending online. I began resenting many people, and I often allowed my day to be ruined by things I read online which were out of my control and outside of my slice of reality. I couldn't make the connection between Twitter and my wellbeing for months and months, but I eventually did. However, during my time in that fog, my mental health was taking hits, and I reacted to this by spending even more time online to escape from the mental health problems, not realising that social media was a main factor in my wellbeing deteriorating.

I thought I couldn't facilitate a successful writing career without it. But this is of course, a load of shite. If you are good enough at something you do not need a social media account to prove it. Donal Ryan and Kevin Barry are two examples of this. People will know well enough if you are really good, and that truisms extends beyond writing. This was simply my excuse to use Twitter more than I should have because I was addicted.

I fell into a dependence on the platform for serotonin and dopamine, and the adverse effects of this comes when you stop getting your hit. If my tweets weren't performing as well as I'd like, it would cause me to feel stress and anxiety at a level too severe to be caused by a social media app on my phone. I obsessed over my tweets, and often deleted them if the engagement was poor. I had become overtly pathetic when it came to my destructive use of this particular social medium. I wanted tweets with big like counts on them, like fat pigs. I kept tabs on who unfollowed me and became quietly obsessed with making sure I got more. It became more than a toxic exercise for me and I continued for months despite my awareness of it, because I was hooked. I wanted clout and to be known, even though I despised these qualities openly. I just couldn't stop myself.

If my desire was truly to just get popular tweets then it would have ousted itself eventually. But that never happened. The real issue was that I wasn't satisfied with my life at that time – I had no real goal or purpose, and felt like I was floating aimlessly without direction – so Twitter became a make-shift escape from a reality I didn't want to face up to. At least if I was thriving on there I didn't have to deal with how I was feeling in the real world.

I eventually deleted the app from my phone in October of 2020, and only used Twitter when I was on my laptop. Although this didn't reduce the number of tweets I made daily, it did stop endless scrolling through my feed, which in fairness, was the primary source of the stress it was causing me. When I couldn't see the hot takes, ignorant views, and angry opinions of the many, I began to feel less distressed in my day-to-day. Once I was able to pull myself away from an utter dependence on the platform, I noticed a reduction in anxiety and an increase in general mood. This development made me uneasy and woke me up to the true impact social media can have. It also made me more understanding of how and why people were enslaved to their Instagram profiles, and how having a false perception of themselves online could make them feel better.

The Lesson

People can be, and are, addicted to social media. I have been one of them. For a long time I blamed the individual person for this, but we don't blame people for being addicted to things like alcohol and heroin, because addiction is a sickness. Social media addiction is no different. Around the time I realised I was addicted, I recall comparing social media use to persistent and daily drug use, and noted that we might one day look back at our collective behaviour and be appalled by our irresponsible use of the online stimulant. I still think that. I will always think that.

Think about this. You've been alone for a long period of time due to a global pandemic that's out of your control. Your mental health is already suffering because you can't see friends and family. You can't fill your free time in the same ways as you could before, so you find yourself online far more often. Doom-scrolling and allowing your undisciplined thoughts to run wild, allowing yourself to share them with others far more often. You get the feel-goods from the validation derived from your complaints and so this becomes your new source of serotonin and dopamine. You slowly complain and become consumed by anger more often over time as you link behaviour to outcome. This happened to thousands of people in 2020. People based their value on it. It made people unreasonable because, instead of having conversations of benefit, you could just rage-tweet and echo-chambers rewarded you for the lack of nuance. You could say the most outrageous things and somewhere out there people would agree with you. It's essential to remember that just because you have an opinion that is supported does not necessarily make this opinion correct. We don't have to rewind too far into the history books to know how true this is.

And so, the antidote to this new unreasonable world, I think, is to be unapologetically reasonable. In a world where the most valued expressions are ones of anger, the rebel is the person who is relentlessly un-angry. Facing up to a lack of nuance with total nuance, facing up to anger with real kindness (not the passive-aggressive kind that came with the 'Be Kind' hashtag), and facing up to begrudgery and disdain with support and compassion are the 'radical' ways to fight back against an increasingly toxic environment.

The lesson here is – be relentlessly good in a world filled with anger and hatred. Meet anger with understanding. Take the higher ground. Don't stoop to the level of the ferocious masses, and don't post things online if you intend to say horrible things about people you don't know.

As Marcus Aurelius once wrote, "Do the right thing. The rest does not matter."

Why Aren't You Happy?

Not so long ago you couldn't go anywhere outside of the country due to a social pressure to act responsibly more so than any restrictions. That is, you could technically still travel internationally, but it was strongly advised that you didn't. As a result, people who did travel were vilified online. The hatred for those few who decided they still deserved a sun holiday during the plight of the pandemic was palpable. Admittedly, I initially joined in on the dogpile. I openly questioned anyone who went abroad, suggesting they were selfish and morally irresponsible. Although those comments might have rung true, moral fortitude was hardly the root of my outcry. Jealousy was far more prominent a motivation for me lashing out. I was sour because I hadn't the gall to head away myself. I was jealous because the level at which I experienced some sort of moral responsibility would have made me guilt ridden if I did head out of the country. Therefore, everyone who did go on holidays was a scoundrel from my biased perspective. I thought I was morally superior to others, and this manifested in a toxic way. I can admit fault there for certain.

I eventually changed my tune on that. By the end of August I had settled into accepting that I was morally conceited. Years previous, when I was 17 and hadn't yet begun to drink, I used to feel morally superior to my fellow peers who did drink (I imagine I was a lot of fun at parties). I looked down on people and judged them for giving into the peer pressure. My brother set me right at the time when he told me I was being self-righteous. He checked me on my bullshit. He told me that just because we believed certain things and acted certain ways, it didn't make them right, universally or otherwise. We didn't know it then, and I doubt he knows it now, but that interaction would forevermore act as a reminder to me to chill the fuck out whenever I got too high up on my horse. Accepting that our opinions and beliefs aren't universally true and are often flawed has become a tenant of my own moral philosophy to this day, and it can be traced back to that night when Cillian fed me a hard truth on our walk up the Ballinlough Road. Being so certain that what we believe is true is a dangerous state of mind to be in, as it breeds division, and an attitude of superiority.

When the reminder came around in 2020, I stopped lashing out at holiday-goers. There were plenty of things we couldn't do that year, many of which made little sense. There were so many nonsensical rules made in a panic, during a global pandemic. You couldn't blame people for getting so sick of it that rules were eventually thrown by the wayside. Eventually we all bent the them, myself included. But that's neither here nor there. As the lockdowns continued to roll in and out like the tide on the worst beach to ever exist, my feelings about what the right thing to do in the situation changed with it. Whereas in the beginning I felt that the rules made sense and that we needed to be in lockdown, towards the end of 2020 I felt almost the opposite. As it turned out, we ended up spending the first half of 2021 in lockdown too, and so it was clear to me for a very long time that lockdowns did not work, at least not in the way they were designed to.

It's an unpopular opinion, and I as understand it, its unpopularity is driven by fear, but lockdowns weren't the answer. They weren't the answer because rather than saving lives, they just traded them. Yes, lockdown saved some people from dying from the virus. I don't doubt that for a second. It took pressure away from the health services and allowed us a better chance at saving the lives of high risk individuals. But lockdown also caused more deaths by virtue of suicide and undiagnosed illnesses due to screenings being halted. Lockdown took away people's livelihoods, and sanity and sense of purpose, so that we might protect ourselves from a disease which we knew very little about. We were living in active fear of the unknown and it was destructive. Lockdown wasn't saving lives, it was just making sure that the lives that were taken weren't taken by COVID-19.

Lockdowns continued to destroy people's mental health. It forced people to become lonely and isolated. Isolation was quite literally encouraged as well as demanded upon. 'Social-isolation' is a term I never wish to hear normalised again. Isolation and alone-ness are dangerous for the vulnerable mind. Being alone when you don't want to be is a difficult position to be in, and it can really affect our wellbeing. This is why solitary confinement is one of the worst punishments in correctional facilities. Humans aren't meant to be alone for prolonged periods – we're social creatures. We're meant to be around one another. That is our biological drive.

Like many, I was very lonely in 2020 and 2021. It was the loneliest period of my life so far. There are many reasons for that. Some of it, as we have seen, was my own doing. Some of it was as a result of the years spent alone up until that point, and how I'd ignored my own issues. I was probably going to feel lonely anyway, but the pandemic exacerbated its intensity. Still, if I hadn't gotten to that place, then I may have never addressed the issues which were causing me to be alone constantly. I would have never acknowledged my emotional unavailability, or my fear of commitment, or the stress I felt, without having felt so lonely.

Life was stripped back to the rudimental things. There were no social gatherings or sporting activities. There was no basketball for me which had always been a massive outlet. There were few distractions from an anxious mind. You couldn't meet people. Dating was almost non-existent and frowned upon. All in all, it was a very isolating time. Without all the intricacies of life to keep me busy, I was forced to spend time with myself. When life is usually at full tilt I welcome alone time to recharge and relax. However, when you're forced to take on more alone time than you'd usually want, when there are no ways to break up the time spent alone, this can have very different consequences. You can get sick of yourself. The difference between solitude and loneliness shows itself again. I had no choice but to be alone. I began to resent being alone, and to dislike my own company.

I remember I'd wake up most mornings dreading the day ahead. There were months where I couldn't draw any joy from life, not the way I used to, at least. Anything that usually brought me happiness felt like a chore. I was constantly tired. I didn't care about anything and my overruling emotions were anxiety, stress and frustration. Small things, things that shouldn't have mattered, set me on a course of stress and poor mood for prolonged afternoons. I felt trapped in my loneliness. I found myself realising that I was burning out around March of 2021. I had no interest in writing anymore. I resented what little writing I was doing. Each time I sat down to put words on paper, they were forced and unnoteworthy. The only alleviation I got was from running, and even that began to feel like too much effort after a full year of doing it.

The problem I had was my reluctance to let anyone know just how lonely I felt. I hid it behind a mask of coping. I was embarrassed by it, which only worked to intensify the feelings I had. Outwardly, I acted like nothing was wrong. If I met people, I was happy and chatty because, well, I was truly delighted to be around people. It was when I found myself alone that I'd deflate like a weather balloon. I'd seep back into the dread and despair, wondering when it would come to an end. I berated myself and told myself I was failing constantly. I felt like there was nothing I could do right in the world. Imagine feeling lonely, and also feeling too ashamed of yourself to be able to share it. That's like swimming away from the lifeboat instead of toward it.

The peak of my loneliness didn't come until very late in the pandemic, around January and February of 2021. I felt the loneliest when lockdown was extended for the third time. This lockdown felt much more unbearable because there was nothing on the horizon. The sense of hope which had existed in previous iterations was gone, and we were left with this feeling that the cycle would never break. Without Christmas to look forward to, we were coming up on a year of dealing with the virus, and things appeared worse than ever. Case numbers were the highest they'd ever been. There seemed to be no end in sight. I spent nearly every day the exact same way. Feeling so flat, so disconnected from anything I really cared about. I often stopped myself from crying. And still, from the outside in, from the perspective of social media and all the rest, I seemed to be driving it on. I appeared to be thriving and taking everything in my stride. I was active and encouraging, but I didn't feel this way. The truth is, I was struggling, and I didn't want to admit it so I pretended I was fine. I rang in the New Year drinking whisky alone. It felt weird and I felt sad. I didn't want to feel this way any longer but I wasn't doing much of anything to pick myself back up. I knew there was an issue to address but instead I was just feeling sorry for myself.

The reason I think this part of my life is important to document is because we tend to think that once we've worked through our problems they'll never come back. I figured I'd defeated loneliness and depression in my early 20s. I didn't think I could succumb to their advances ever again. I was totally wrong about that. You never become immune to mental health issues. They don't just disappear forever because you've shaken off the grips of them once. You just learn about yourself, and how to cope better. You learn what works for you and you learn what makes things worse. With that information you can do a lot to fortify yourself, but you can't immunise completely from mental health problems.

Relationships and good social supports are ways of doing this. I'm not saying I didn't have good social supports either, I had plenty of people to lean on. Plenty of people who cared for me and whom I cared for too. I just felt too ashamed of myself to open up. I felt like everyone had enough going on without having to deal with my self-pity spiral. So my mental health deteriorated because I got complacent, and I stayed poorly because I wouldn't ask for help. I was convinced I could no longer suffer from depression and anxiety so I stopped proactively maintaining my mental health.

The guilt and shame compounded my isolation and I felt like there was no way out of it. And yet I knew that I wanted things to change. I didn't want to continue to prolong my suffering.

I knew there was a perspective issue causing me to feel so alone. I didn't want to keep looking elsewhere when happiness could be found right in front of me if I let it. I wanted to stop making excuses for myself. I knew then that I was done with being emotionally unavailable and alone and angry. My unwillingness to address all of the issues discussed throughout these essays was the reason I found myself alone. I wanted to share my life with someone else. I wanted to sacrifice my time for them. I have been so reluctant to give up any time to anyone before. So I wanted to look at myself and try to improve, because the way I was going was destructive, and it was only going to get worse. I wanted to improve my relationship with myself so that I could in turn, improve my relationships with others.

The Lesson

In 2021 I learned something very important. Something that had been holding me back for years. I wasn't allowing myself to be happy. Deep down, under all my excuses and bullshit, I believed that I didn't deserve to be happy. I felt that I was an imposter. I felt intense survivor's guilt. I couldn't be happy because I wouldn't let myself be, and I wouldn't let myself be, because on some level, I no longer liked the person I was. I was fighting with myself for years without any knowledge of it. I refused to see the reality of what was going on, so instead, I blamed other people for my own issues. I told myself that people couldn't understand me, and that it was their problem and not mine.

I was tired.

I was tired of not allowing myself to feel anything. I wanted to feel things. I wanted to be happy. I wanted to experience life through a lens that wasn't numb disassociation. But in order to do that, you have to understand why you subconsciously won't allow yourself to be happy. So that became a priority. I decided that I needed to understand why I was keeping the possibility of happiness away from myself, because I knew the loneliness I had always felt was a result of this denial.

Sunlight Through The Curtains

M any of us don't allow ourselves to be happy until some arbitrary point in the 'future' which, of course, never arrives.

We say things like, *"I'll be happy when I get this job,"* or, *"I'll be happy when I get this house"*, or, *"Once I have this much money I'll be happy."* It's never ending. The goalposts are constantly moving onto the next unattainable desire. When we exist like this, we're guaranteeing to ourselves that we'll never really and truly be happy. There'll always be something else to achieve, or something else to buy. There is no upper limit when we view happiness like this. This is no way to attain satisfaction. To be genuinely happy you have to find a way to appreciate that which you already have. This is wisdom that's been passed down through the centuries, from the times of Marcus Aurelius to the present day:

"Do not indulge in dreams of having what you have not, but reckon up the chief of the blessings you do possess, and then thankfully remember how you would crave for them if they were not yours."

To find peace, we have to get to a point where the life we currently live is enough for us to be happy. I think we know this subconsciously, but it's a very hard mindset to actively engage in, because we find it difficult to not want more.

Our world is often one shaped by individualist thought; think about the world with yourself at the centre, chase individual achievements, ambitions and desires. This culture of ours breeds innovation and mind-blowing progress, but it also instils a sensation of being on a treadmill, where nothing will ever be enough. Where there will always be more needed doing in order to attain this arbitrary happiness.

I've always felt like I've been looking in on my life from the outside, as if it were a snow globe. I could see the moments passing by like blurry snowflakes, but I never found a way to engage them. It's never felt like I ever got the hang of what came so naturally to others. Over the years, I've watched as people found happiness right in front of them. I've seen people find good relationships, and create lives that bring them joy. I've watched as people got on with their lives whilst I continued to feel stuck. There has been a certain effortlessness to the way people live that I have been unable to fully understand. It has never felt like I could make things work so well, and for it come to me so naturally. I've always been searching for more, and it's always felt like being present and happy in my life takes far more effort than it does for others.

I've wondered over the past few years why I couldn't just be happy with what I have right now like most people can. It's why I wrote this book. I've been trying for as long as I can remember to break into my own life and actually live it. I've been watching myself from the other side of the glass, critiquing my every move, and shouting abuse at myself whenever I make even the smallest mistake. I've been the voice telling me all the awful things I've believed about who I am, and at a certain point you have to cut ties with that voice.

For most of my adult life (I've only been an adult for a decade or so!) I've told myself quietly and firmly that happiness isn't something I deserve. I was never good enough for happiness, like I was too bad to deserve it. I'm still not certain where this stems from, but I do know that it is a pertinent part of why low mood, and loneliness have been my defaults – I believed that a lonely existence was the only existence I was entitled to. In The Merchant of Venice, Antonio says that the world is *"a stage where every man must play a part, and mine a sad one."* Somewhere in me, that resonated when I read it all the way back at age fifteen, and it somehow became true – in my head at least – that my role must also be the sad one. There was no way around it, and so long stints of happiness have always been out of reach and out of question. I confirmed my own prophecy over the years, as each stint of loneliness became evidence that I was destined to be this way.

It's been a challenge to address this and come to terms with it. It's something I've never told anyone, really. I've been working against myself for almost a decade, ensuring that I would never draw consistent happiness from anything. Up until now I haven't given myself permission to be happy. Happiness has always been something only other people deserved. This subconscious belief has led to many acts of self-sabotage. Again, and again I have ruined good things for myself, things that would have brought me happiness if I let go of the fears, and allowed myself to live without guilt. I've thrown away relationships. I've acted destructively. I've been toxic. All as a result of this idea, this whisper in the night, that I do not deserve to be happy. But why has some hidden part of me believed that I don't deserve happiness? That's a tricky question to answer.

The problem, I think, is that I've conceptualised my own personal happiness as something to be earned. It is something I have to work to deserve, and because I've always struggled with the idea of being a morally bad person, it never really felt like I earned this happiness. As long as I believe that I am bad I will never think I deserve good things. However, this is a standard I have held solely for myself. I've never thought that anyone else had to earn their share. I knew everyone else deserved happiness unconditionally wherever they could find it, but I was the one person that had to earn it. Once again, the bar I held for myself was slippery and unreachable. And so, in my mind I have to work and grind and struggle for my happiness, which means that whenever happiness came my way I shunned it, because I didn't feel I had earned it yet. I felt that I hadn't done enough work to make up for 'badness' in me, and so, once more, the goalposts were moved repeatedly.

Much like the other unquantifiable markers for happiness – the attainment of wealth, the houses, and the rest – there was no fixed definition for what *'earning my happiness'* even meant. I have no metrics to measure this. There was no set of time in which I saw this coming to a conclusion. There was no way to track it whatsoever, which meant that if I kept going along the path I was on with the mindset I had, I would spend the rest of my life trying to earn something which was unearnable. It was to be a Sisyphean struggle – like he who was condemned by the Greek gods to push a rock up a hill for eternity, I constantly looked to earn my happiness, yet would never be satisfied enough to grant myself the reward I craved. Nothing I could do, no matter how noble or impactful, was ever enough for me to be happy. I wasn't aiming at anything in particular. My definition of what happiness is was vague and hidden, and you can't aim at things you cannot see.

Yet, if I switched my perspective, if I shook the fog from my head, it would have become clear that happiness isn't something one deserves or not. Happiness is accepting who you are, and where you are, and knowing that it's good enough. It has nothing to do with achievements of status or wealth. In fact, I'd argue that the more one concerns themselves with these sorts of material endeavours, the less likely they are to become happy. I was so focused on pushing forward, and always aiming at the future, that I wasn't living in the present. I neglected everything in the now – my feelings, my relationships, my contentment – because I was so obsessed with being happy further down the line. But that future never comes. The day where you will eventually be happy never arrives because you will always only experience the present. And so if I continue down this path, it will be impossible to find the happiness I seek.

This has been my real issue then. This is the root source of every other problem – the depression, the production guilt, the jealousy, the anxiety – all of it stemmed from the belief that I wasn't good enough. The root of my inability to be satisfied with anything in my life was that I had a poor relationship with myself. I did not like myself. and there's no hope for us to build other more successful relationships if we can't even build a healthy one with ourselves. It makes total sense to feel lonely when you don't even like who you are. That's about as lonely a place as you can be. I couldn't be happy so long as I failed to mend the relationship I had with myself. The worst part of all is I didn't know I held contempt towards myself until 2021.

I never actually sat myself down and forgave myself. Every mistake I've ever made just worked as proof that I was a bad person. Every relationship I've short-changed, every harsh thing I've ever said, every time I've behaved poorly – this was the evidence. And I never forgave myself for any of it. Instead, I held all my shortcomings against myself, and told myself I could never be happy because of the bad things I have done. I never forgave myself for the guilt I felt after Erbie died. I never forgave myself for becoming emotionally unavailable. I never forgave myself for a thousand different things. This become the foundation for the relationship I have with myself – and that is a very rotten place to begin from.

What does feeling like you're not worthy of happiness look like? I suppose it's different for everyone. For me it was a lot of work. Working constantly to try and prove that I could become good enough. I overachieved in everything. I was relentless in a lot of ways. Whether it was school or college or writing or sport – I was always doing something, not out of a sense of purpose, but out of a fear of being mediocre. Of course, being busy and driven isn't a bad thing, objectively, but it can be if the reasons for your drive are corrupted. I was driven because I felt like if I wasn't productive constantly then that made me 'bad'. It made me bad because I believed I was wasting my time if I wasn't always working. That's poisonous. You wouldn't treat a friend like this, but it felt totally okay to treat myself with such disregard.

The ironic thing is that I imagine this drive to work has made me look well-adjusted and content from the outside looking in. Especially during the long bouts when I couldn't work up the courage to talk openly about how I was really feeling. From outside it probably just looked as though I was focused on whatever task was at hand. I never had time to spare because there was always something to be done. Yet in my mind, I was just trying to prove myself worthy of happiness. It was as if I was trying to scrub out the stains of guilt so that one day down the line I'd be allowed to feel happy.

On top of this, whenever I did achieve something, it never gave me any lasting sense of satisfaction, which further compounded the idea that I couldn't be happy. As soon as one thing was acknowledged, or a result was achieved, or an award was won, my focus moved to the next thing. There was no solace to be found in success. The work was a medium to earn my happiness, but even when the moment for happiness did eventually arrive, I wouldn't allow myself to feel it. Happiness is virtually unattainable if you view it through this lens.

Finding Meaning

It's worth noting that I was placing far too much emphasis on the role happiness plays in life satisfaction, too. For a long time I believed happiness to be the meaning of life, but now I don't think that's entirely accurate. If we can achieve happiness in the moments where it can be derived, well and good. Happiness is rare and fleeting, so it should be enjoyed where and when we can find it. However, our satisfaction with life comes from having an appropriate purpose and reasonable responsibility, more so than it does from instant gratification and pleasure. How many people claim that they would continue to work if they suddenly became wealthy? How many cautionary tales are there about want-for-nothings with too much free time and nothing to strive for? We know at an instinctive level that happiness isn't the meaning of our lives, although it is a worthwhile feeling to attain if you can.

Our sense of meaning comes from having something worthwhile to do every day, which gives us justifiable reasons to get out of bed. This can, and often does, lead to happiness in the long-term. The purpose presupposes the satisfaction, though, which explains why long-lasting happiness is rarely found in lives without purpose, or ones dedicated to chasing short-term pleasures and following the path of least resistance.

And perhaps this is why I couldn't find happiness in my early to mid-twenties. I didn't have something that gave me this sense of purpose. My day job didn't make me feel this way. I adored writing, but the industry seemed so competitive in a time where people aren't overly enthused about publishing men, that it felt like an unrealistic ask to want this as a career path. The era we live in demands that there are additional barriers to being published in an attempt to correct wrong-doings of the past. I understand why this is, of course, but it also caused my hope of getting published to dwindle. So I had no sense of real purpose. I sought short term relationships for pleasure rather than making the necessary sacrifices to find a more meaningful one. And so, if we really get into it, it wasn't so much that I wouldn't allow myself to find happiness, it was that I felt lost, without a sense of purpose, and I couldn't be happy without knowing I was doing something which had a meaning.

All of this is apparent now because I've spent time reflecting and working through all the painful shite, but I couldn't see any of these behaviours for what there were for most of my life. I had an undisciplined mind with no sense of purpose which kept defending itself from what was really happening. My happiness was being denied because I wasn't doing all of the things I ought to be doing in order to live a more meaningful life. I was moving from short-term fix to short-term fix without realising my issue required a more long-term solution. If the relationship I had with myself was better, I think it would have been easier for me to do the right things. I would have stopped working against myself. I wouldn't have made myself feel guilty about everything. I wouldn't have felt like a bad person for behaving like everyone else did. I would have been able to find a relationship and stay in it because I wouldn't have been fighting with myself the entire time.

It's been difficult to understand this part of who I am, but it has been the Holy Grail of flaw realisations. Like all the other flaws I 've become aware of over the past number of years – the self-sabotaging, the emotional unavailability – knowing of their existence simply isn't enough to make them disappear. What's more is that nearly every other flaw I've discovered can be traced back to this parent issue of having no purpose and not accepting happiness in the present. You can't just close your eyes and wish for problems to go away, which is what I've been doing for quite some time. I'd love if it were that easy. There would be no period of painful acceptance if you could just flip a switch.

The real work comes after the realisation. The real work is noticing the behaviour when it's happening and stopping yourself from engaging in the moment. The healing, so to speak, comes from being mindful of the infection. And so, my work began with understanding that my lack of satisfaction, and the loneliness I felt, all stemmed from a lack of passion for my life, because I couldn't find my purpose within it. This lack of passion came from the poor relationship I had with myself, and this in turn can explain why I couldn't get satisfaction from anything, because I told myself I didn't – and would never – deserve to be happy.

And so, I began to notice that I was feeling nothing when I could be feeling something. I stopped overlooking the small wins and forced myself to appreciate them. Instead of passing over all the moments which could bring happiness, I began to over emphasise the impact of every moment. A lot of this specific realisation has come from death anxiety. I harnessed this fear, and each day I tell myself that one day I will no longer exist, and to take any of these small things for granted is the work of a fool. Doing this every day has made a huge difference in my mindset, my perspective, and indeed my level of satisfaction.

Taking Aim At The Road Ahead

For years I felt guilt for being alive after my friend died. It didn't seem fair. It still doesn't seem fair, but I no longer feel bad for being alive. That was a reaction to combat the shame of thinking I let him down on that Wednesday afternoon. I know now that I didn't let him down. Letting someone down implies a level of knowledge or understanding of a situation and still acting incorrectly. But I didn't know what was going on with him, so I couldn't have let him down.

We can't control everything. We can't even control **most** of what happens, but we can always control how we behave after things happen. When we use traumatic events to create parts of our identity we're telling ourselves over and over to not move on from them. That's an attachment issue, really. For me, the fallout of not being able to move on was a numbness. I was afraid to feel anything to that extent again. The pain was too much, so I reacted by becoming numb to everything. I went too far down the road of unattachment to ensure that I could never get hurt that badly again. But that's not how life works. Instead of never feeling that bad again, I began to feel that bad constantly. I numbed myself to positive emotions and only felt negative ones. Loneliness is an open wound, and it is one that I kept open as a result of not dealing with my grief properly. I was trying to heal myself by doing more damage. There's no rhyme or reason to that. Instead of successfully feeling no pain, I couldn't feel anything in great depths. Any happiness I felt was dying embers instead of a full-on raging fire.

And when I stepped back and finally saw all of this, it is no wonder my relationships never worked. At the same time I wanted them to work, but was also working to ensure they never would. I was convinced that I was better on my own, yet whenever I was alone I felt isolated and sad. What a tragic cycle that is. Looking for companionship yet making sure that no woman could ever stay around long enough for the relationship to work. It was a form of self-torture in essence. I dangled what I wanted most of all in front of myself like a carrot on a stick.

For the longest time I didn't even realise that I was the architect of it all. My self-destructive path resulted in a lot of damage by proxy. My issues weren't just affecting me. They rippled and affected other people. Instead of sharing the load and healing, I was passing on the hurt to others. It emanated out from me, and I know that I hurt some people deeply. I can't undo the harm I caused but I can, and have, tried to learn from it.

When I step back and take an honest look at myself now, I see a man who is scared. He is scared of failing. He is scared of being alone, and of not being good enough. He is scared of waking up one day and realising that he screwed it all up. There is certainly a lot of fear. Until quite recently, I have never acknowledged this fear. I buried it deep, and I pretended that no fear existed within me. This didn't eradicate the fear, but it changed the way it looked. Before it surfaced in my mind as certainty – certainty that I would fail, and die alone, and push everyone away in the end. Instead of fearing that I was a bad person, I began to believe I was one. My life has been a series of running away from these fears, these things I believed to be certainties, hoping that I could outrun them eventually and fall into happiness without addressing any of the fears and problems.

It's strange how everything begins to click once you know the source of the pain. Like a jigsaw, these things are easier to make sense of once the bigger picture is in front of you. I remember once myself and my mother tried to do a jigsaw with no idea of what the final picture would look like and it took weeks. We stood over that thing, unable to figure out what was going on because we couldn't see all the parts. A similar thing occurred to me with my mental health – I couldn't see what was going wrong because I refused to look upon the full picture.

Admitting to myself that I was withholding my own happiness has been the hardest thing to do, because it means that I've been in the villain in my own story. I tortured myself. I've put relentless pressure on myself and held myself to unrealistic standards. And all of this was an obstacle course set up by yours truly. Making it through to the happiness on the other side of it was an impossible task.

This embargo on happiness manifests most prominently in the different varieties of guilt I've always felt. Guilt for being alive while Erbie was dead. Guilt for not being productive enough. Guilt for not being good enough. Guilt felt any time I was having fun. Guilt for being sexually active. The list goes one. All of these were signs that I was subconsciously judging myself for trying to live. Not allowing myself to exist like everyone else does without feeling some sort of guilt is a non-stop form of torture. Life is hard enough without feeling guilty about the way you live it. Every move I've ever made has been met with some variation of guilt.

My next move then, is to try and reduce these levels of guilt. Once I learn to accept that some guilt is normal and that a lot of it can be ignored, then it will be time to find something and aim wholeheartedly at it. This thing – this passion – will allow me to find daily meaning. We need that to live well, I think – a sense of purpose. A sense that what we are doing is worthwhile. And I believe that I have already found that in mental health work and writing, if only I could put everything I am into it. Up until now, I've aimed half-heartedly because I didn't think I deserved to do what I've wanted to do. There has been a lack of self-belief, perhaps because this road is difficult and full of rejection and very, very long. But it's worth trying. I think we crave a difficult road. The road that is cleared away for us and easy to walk down doesn't give us this sense of accomplishment and purpose that we require in order to be happy.

Even the road so far – the one where I have looked upon my flaws and tried to grow from them – has been difficult and painful, but it has brought me closer to who I really am, and therefore has been totally worthwhile. This path has led me to a place where I can finally forgive myself.

The road which challenges us is the road we must seek out, rather than the path of least resistance.

So, now I must aim at the difficult road ahead, knowing that there is more pain there for me, but also knowing that the pain is bearable, and will be worthwhile in the end. If I can do that, then slowly the purpose I crave, and the happiness I seek will slip in like sunlight through the curtains on a summer's morning, and I'll know then that I have forgiven myself for years of neglect.

Final Words

I don't have all the answers. In fact, I have very few.

I will never have them all and I could never claim to have them all. I'm not currently a qualified mental health professional. I can't tell you exactly what works and doesn't work and neither can many mental health professionals, as research on the brain has continued to exponentially grow over the past couple of decades. I can't tell you what you should and should not do for your mental health. Even if I somehow knew these things I would never assume to know what works for you better than you do. That knowledge is personal and is different for all of us.

I am just a man who has had mental health problems, ones that may plague a lot of people, and I decided to write them all down as I worked through them. I have no special skillset in this arena. What I do have is experience, a penchant for articulating things which are difficult to articulate, and an ability to critique myself. What I also have is an ability to see when there is a problem within me. This has been invaluable, but I haven't always been able to do this. It takes a lot of painful reflection and time to become aware of ourselves. It takes seeing who we are underneath all the defence mechanisms and idiosyncrasies. And most of the time, we are the scared children of our childhoods trying to make it up as we go along. Life becomes a little less daunting, and you become a little more gentle when you perceive everyone in this light.

Understanding why we behave the way we do is tricky and we often get it wrong. I have no doubt that some of my best guesses at what causes me to behave in the ways I do are misled, or at least not the full picture. We're a very new species, relatively speaking, and we have many abilities that no other species in existence has. One such ability is to be able to explain things retroactively. We can reach far back into our lives and attach intentions, motivations, emotions, and conclusions to blurry memories of events. This is a powerful ability and one that can be easily used irresponsibly or inaccurately. It's far too easy to stretch back and attach emotions that weren't actually present at the time.

There are parts of my college years I look back on now with a sense of deep-rooted sadness, but it is unlikely that I felt this way at the time. I only attach sadness now because I understand I was ignoring the pain I was feeling. So we must be careful with this, because rewriting our pasts can cause more damage than anything. You can paint yourself in a light that isn't true, convince yourself of mental health problems that didn't exist, and draw conclusions for which there is no real evidence. You can frame your life in a totally negative light if you aren't careful, and this can distort your own idea of who you are. Particularly in a world that obsesses over labels, it is easy to look into the past and paint traumas and attach labels that were never there to begin with.

Reflecting is essential, I think, to be able to live a well-rounded and moral life. This book opens with the words of Seneca regarding this. We must reflect but we must not embellish or exaggerate or distort, because then we are attempting to grow from a place which doesn't exist. You cannot grow flowers from a rainbow; you must grow them from the ground.

Confronting our flaws and maladaptive habits is no easy task. In fact, it's very painful. It unearths truths about ourselves that we would rather not know. The easier path is the path where we fill our lives with distractions and things that don't have real value to prevent ourselves from addressing these problems. However, easy does not equal right. Things that are worthwhile are often ones that are difficult to obtain. If addressing our flaws is hard then it logically follows that it is a worthwhile endeavour.

Let no parts of yourself lurk in the darkness. Seek them out and know them, so that you are never caught off guard by the more monstrous parts of you. Learn how to deal with the parts you don't like, improve the parts that can be improved, and fortify the parts of yourself which you already enjoy and love. This is a daily, consistent effort that will often feel futile. It is only when you look back and reflect that you will see exactly how far you have come, and how much more of yourself that you truly and deeply know.

I've spent a great amount of time on my own. Not all of it has been lonely, but some of it has been. This loneliness forced me to address the reasons why I found myself in this position. This reflection was challenging but deeply relieving in a far more life-changing way. I now understand myself in a way I never have before, and I think there's something in this. Our oldest stories often recant stories of people lost in the desert, or in the jungle, alone and helpless, only to return with a deep sense of purpose and understanding. Think of Jesus, Moses, even Luke Skywalker. There is something valuable in going through an ordeal alone and coming back out on the other side. The hero's journey – Hercules, Homer, Gilgamesh, Spider-Man – every example includes an extended period of struggle, doubt and fear before the hero (that's you) fully understands who they are, and thus, prevails.

There is value in loneliness, despite its adverse effects. But this value is only found if you look for it rather than curl up into a ball of self-pity and continue to blame the world for your own shortcomings.

The work is never finished.

Throughout all of this, I think that is the most important take away. You are never done with working on yourself. You never get to a point where you become immune to mental health problems. There are times when your mental health is very good and it *feels* like there is no way you could ever crumble again. And then there are times where it feels like you'll never be able to pick yourself back up.

Looking back, it's nearly always when I feel my mental health is impenetrable that I begin to fall. It's always at times when I get complacent – when I'm spending too much time alone, or too much time on social media unchecked, or ignoring my mental health routine – during these times is when I begin to struggle. That seems obvious now but it isn't so obvious when you're in the middle of it. When we stop working on ourselves we begin to disimprove. I suppose that's the nature of our universe and our reality. Things begin to decay and fall apart over time. Mental health is no different. Good and consistent mental health isn't just luck of the draw, it takes effortful and disciplined work. I didn't understand this myself for years.

We all do things which harm our mental health, and we often do these things on purpose because we think they'll bring us happiness. And for a brief time, they do bring us some enjoyment, and thrill, but these choices rarely align with happiness. Drinking, and taking drugs, and having casual sex, and all the rest of the thing we do for hedonistic pleasure – when we do these things too often they wreak havoc on our mental health.

It's hard to make the right choices. Often the right thing to do is not what we would prefer to do. Sometimes we don't want to get enough sleep or drink enough water. Sometimes we want to get drunk and stay out all night. This is where the discipline of mental health kicks in. Doing the best thing for ourselves won't always be the most enjoyable thing. Going to the doctor isn't ever fun, but it's sometimes what you need to do for your own wellbeing. It's no easy feat to be able to take care of yourself the way you ought to, because it means you have to say no to yourself sometimes and that can be difficult. Real self-care is taking responsibility for yourself in this way.

It is doing the things you are avoiding doing, rather than taking the easy road every single time.

So, in this sense, working on our mental health is a constant grind. The same way that you work out every day so that you can look a certain way, you must work on your mental health every day in order to feel a certain way. We're never taught to think like this about our mental wellbeing as children, but it's an incredibly important and empowering way to frame mental health. You have the power to heal your mind, and all it takes is consistent and diligent work every day. I'm not saying this to you from any sort of hilltop, either. It's very difficult to maintain this level of discipline constantly. What I'm saying is, I know now that my own mental health takes a hit when I'm struggling with this ability to self-control. When I fall out of discipline I fall into anxiety and low mood. Even as I wrote this book I fell into several undisciplined periods. I drank too often and I made bad decisions because of this drinking. I spent many days in self-contempt loops, constantly listening to the voice telling me that I was worthless, and that I was a bad person.

When you get so far with your mental health, and you have seen real progress, it can be devastating when you fall back into disrepair. Not only are you dealing with whatever symptoms of poor mental health that emerge, you additionally deal with a degree of guilt because you feel like you've failed in some way. For me, struggling mentally has always had the bonus feature of making me feel ashamed of myself. I feel like I have let myself down, and this only makes matters worse.

Stigma can be really tricky. It's difficult to stop yourself from feeling a certain way. You can't just switch it off. I know full well that feeling ashamed for being in a low period makes little sense, but that doesn't make the shame disappear. It takes far more effort to get over something like that, and this effort takes time. Now, when I get into a low period, there is no shame because I've learned to see these low points in a different way. These bad spells are a sign that I need to change something in my life, because it is solely the way I have been behaving and living that has caused me to fall into a depression.

We need that sense of discipline, and the reassurance that we are acting in a way that is conducive with our own contentment. Drinking every weekend isn't conducive with contentment for me, for example. Although it brings me immediate joy and euphoria because I enjoy the time with my friends, it does more damage in the aftermath than you would consider worthwhile. And so the more I engage with this behaviour, the higher the risk of my mental health deteriorating.

These are the types of things we all do which we know to be bad for us in the long-term but bring us comfort in the short-term. We think we're doing the right thing but we're not. It's an act of self-harm in a sense, to constantly engage in behaviours that destroy us. Yet, in our world it's totally normalised. We all do it, and we convince ourselves that it is okay because everyone else is doing it, too. We march into sickness with everyone else because we're afraid to say no to our urges and desires. We don't want to delay gratification because that means we'll have to face up to our flaws and our problems and the things that hurt. Our flaws are plentiful, and our ability to ignore them is unbound.

This is why the work is never complete. There is always more we can do to get better. It is not enough to just have good mental health now. We need to behave so that we have good mental health now, and tomorrow, and in ten years from now. Doing this takes work and so we need to be responsible and get busy.

Think of you as you exist now, and all the future versions of you, as a community. Think of this group as one which relies on you, because they do, and what you do today will have lasting effects on this group. So we ought to do things that best serve this group – which includes you. The community of you depends on you, and so only looking after your present self's mental health is not enough. You still have work to do for the future of your mental health, and so do I.

I remember as I finished this book, I stood in the kitchen of my parents' home one evening in June and I spoke with my mother. She feels that looking inward all the time is playing with fire. And it is. It can be dangerous, and it can be painful. It may not even be for everyone. But I told her then, as we stood there with the sun falling from the sky through the window, that I had an inexplicable feeling that looking inward and trying to understand who exactly I am feels like purpose. It feels like something worthwhile to do with my life, even if it doesn't always bring about instant happiness.

And the reason I think looking inward is worthwhile is because it's a constant effort, a well that never runs dry, because there is always more you can learn about yourself, and through this mechanism, you can learn about the people and the world around you. By doing this you can try to help others figure themselves out, too.

The work is never finished – that seems like a pretty good place to begin.

Be good,
Daragh

Acknowledgments:

Right, here's the most important and most difficult part of the book to write, primarily because there is an almost infinite number of people to thank.

I'd first like to thank everyone at Book Hub Publishing, namely the Director and Commissioning Editor, Susan McKenna and her review team. Also, Niall MacGiolla Bhuí from TheDocCheck.Com for believing in this book and taking it from a hopeful manuscript to bookshelf. I needed a publisher who cared about this book as much as I do, and our first meeting in Limerick told me all I needed to know about your passion.

Thank you to Jason O'Gorman, fellow Corkonian and incredible talent, who designed and created a beautiful cover for the book. Thank you also to Conor Stone, a dear friend who read *Lonely Boy* in the very early stages and provided encouragement and suggestions which helped to make this book the best version it could be.

On the subject of encouragement, I'd like to thank the wider Irish writing community. There are so many who provided sincere and essential words of encouragement. People like Louise Nealon, Anne Griffin, Amanda Geard, Olivia Fitzsimons, Tadhg Coakley, Patrick Holloway, Lauren O'Donovan, Róisín Leggett Bohan, Lucy Holme-Roberts, JP McHugh, Faye Proctor, Lizzy Shortall, Patrick Osborne – the list goes on – without the welcoming and encouraging friends in this community it would have been far more difficult to write anything at all.

Thank you to my friends, many of whom make up a group called *The Lonely Boys*, for understanding why I needed to write such a book and encouraging me the entire time, throughout this project, and always. It is difficult to doubt yourself with such unyielding support.

Thank you to Karen Underwood for allowing me to write candidly about your son, Erbie, who was my very best friend and someone I miss dearly every single day.

A huge thank you must be made to everyone who has ever read, encouraged and engaged with *Thoughts Too Big* over the years. This blog has been a wellspring of salvation for me, and hopefully it has helped some of you, too.

Thank you to each and every editor, reader, reviewer, and person who has ever published, supported, accepted, rejected and given time to anything I've written. Without you there'd be nowhere to put words (and also nothing to complain about).

And finally, thank you to my family for your patience and understanding. Thank you for putting up with the many mood swings and tantrums throughout the writing of this book and in general. Ye have a lot to put up with in fairness. It goes without saying that every book, story, or scrap of writing is dedicated to you, my parents, Catherine and Paul, and my brother, Cillian.

None of it would exist without such a wellspring of support, nor would it exist without the generosity of you, the reader – thank you for taking the time to read, and thank you for taking the time to understand.

Endorsements

"The future of mental health advocacy is safe in the hands of Daragh Fleming. This generation can finally destroy the stigma that did its very best to try to destroy my generation. Daragh has been a god send to A Lust For Life, injecting huge energy into our mission." – **Niall Breslin, Co-founder of youth mental health charity A Lust For Life**

"Daragh Fleming is doing Trojan work in transcribing the emotional pain that has been lying dormant and stubbornly silent in men for generations. This book has the capacity to save lives. It is an extraordinary testament to a dear friend." – **Louise Nealon, bestselling author of *Snowflake***

"A book of great depth and honesty. Nothing is held back for which I was truly thankful. There is much learning here for all of us." – **Anne Griffin, author of *When All Is Said***

"Lonely Boy is a beautifully-written triumph: prescribed reading in our endless quest for meaning. For me, the pages of a great non-fiction book are a mirror; your own anxieties reflected back at you, your outlook an echo to the words. I think it's safe to say that Lonely Boy will truly resonate and – wonderfully – succeed in making countless readers infinitely less alone." – **Amanda Geard, author of *The Midnight House***

"Lonely Boy is a stunning achievement and such an important book for the times we live in. In his exploration of mental health, relationships, loneliness and loss, Daragh Fleming has done us all a great service. The book is brave, insightful, reflective and moving. His deft blend of the personal and universal makes the essays very readable, but the writing is also skilful and vivid. By confronting his demons and his injurious behaviour in his late teens and twenties, he has produced a book that many will associate with and that many should read – a rare feat." – **Tadhg Coakley, author of *The Game***

Printed in Great Britain
by Amazon